I0119639

Anonymous

# Revised Regulations for the Government of the United States Marine-Hospital Service

Anonymous

**Revised Regulations for the Government of the United States Marine-Hospital Service**

ISBN/EAN: 9783337162801

Printed in Europe, USA, Canada, Australia, Japan

Cover: Foto ©ninafisch / pixelio.de

More available books at **www.hansebooks.com**

# REVISED REGULATIONS

# THE GOVERNMENT

OF THE

# UNITED STATES MARINE-HOSPITAL SERVICE.

———— ◄►► ————

## APPROVED APRIL 24, 1885.

———— ◄►► ————

WASHINGTON:
GOVERNMENT PRINTING OFFICE
1885.

TREASURY DEPARTMENT,
Document No. 695.
Marine-Hospital Service.

# TREASURY DEPARTMENT,

## OFFICE OF THE SUPERVISING SURGEON-GENERAL,

### U. S. MARINE-HOSPITAL SERVICE,

*Washington, D. C., April* 24, 1885.

The following Regulations for the government of the United States Marine-Hospital Service are hereby adopted, and will be enforced from and after the 1st day of July, 1885.

All regulations and circulars, hitherto in operation, which are inconsistent or in conflict with these regulations are hereby repealed.

JOHN B. HAMILTON,

*Supervising Surgeon-General, U. S. M.-H. S.*

Approved :

DANIEL MANNING,

*Secretary of the Treasury.*

Approved :

GROVER CLEVELAND.

# CONTENTS.

## APPENDIX.

# ORGANIZATION.

# ORGANIZATION.

1. The corps of the United States Marine-Hospital Service shall consist of the Supervising Surgeon-General, surgeons, passed assistant surgeons, assistant surgeons, subordinate officers, and employés.

Organization.

## SUPERVISING SURGEON-GENERAL.

2. The Supervising Surgeon-General is charged by law with the supervision, under the direction of the Secretary of the Treasury, of all matters connected with the Marine-Hospital Service and with the disbursement of the marine-hospital fund. The medical officers and acting assistant surgeons will receive their orders from the Supervising Surgeon-General.

Supervising Surgeon-General of the Marine-Hospital Service.

29 June, 1870, c. 169, s. 6, v. 16, p. 170.
3 Mar., 1875, c. 130, v. 18, p. 377.

3. The Supervising Surgeon-General will prepare and revise, subject to the approval of the Secretary of the Treasury, all regulations and instructions for the government of the officers and employés of the Marine-Hospital Service.

To prepare and revise regulations.

4. The Supervising Surgeon-General will exercise constant vigilance over officers and employés of the Service, and will cause prompt and impartial investigation to be made of any reported dereliction of duty.

To supervise officers and employés.

5. The Supervising Surgeon-General will cause the property returns of medical officers and acting assistant surgeons of the Marine-Hospital Service to be examined, and take care that all public property is duly accounted for.

To care for public property.

## MEDICAL CORPS.

6. Medical officers in the Marine-Hospital Service will be appointed by the Secretary of the Treasury, upon the recommendation of the Supervising Surgeon-General, after an examination as to their qualifications as hereinafter provided.

Appointment in medica corps.

7. Original appointments of medical officers in the United States Marine-Hospital Service will be made to the grade of assistant surgeon only.

Original appointments.

Qualifications for appointment.

8. No person will be appointed an assistant surgeon whose age is less than twenty-one or more than thirty years, and, as a preliminary to a recommendation for appointment, the applicant must have graduated in medicine at some respectable medical college, and must pass a satisfactory physical and professional examination before a board of surgeons of the Marine-Hospital Service, which will be convened, from time to time, for that purpose, by the Secretary of the Treasury.

Subject to change of station.

9. Medical officers in the Marine-Hospital Service will not be appointed to any particular station, but to the general service, subject to change of station, as the exigencies of the Service may require, and shall serve in any part of the United States wherever assigned to duty.

## EXAMINATIONS.

Successful examination does not insure appointment.

10. The passing of an examination will not be considered as giving assurance of appointment, as the Department will select those of the highest attainments in case there should be more candidates than vacancies.

Candidates qualified, eligible for one year.

11. No qualified candidate will be eligible for appointment more than one year. If not appointed within that time, he may, if he desires, be re-examined, when, if successful, he will take position with the class last examined.

Unsuccessful applicants may be re-examined.

12. An applicant failing at one examination may be allowed a second examination, after one year, but not a third.

Promotion of assistant surgeons.

13. Assistant surgeons, after three years' service, shall be entitled to an examination for promotion to the grade of passed assistant surgeon. The application for this examination must be accompanied with testimonials of correct deportment and habits of industry from the surgeons with whom they have served, and the applicant must be familiar with these regulations, and must also certify that he is physically able for service in any climate.

Promotion of passed assistant surgeons.

14. A vacancy in the grade of surgeon will be filled by promotion from among the passed assistant surgeons, who shall be eligible for promotion to the grade of surgeon in the order of seniority, but they will not be promoted until they shall have passed a satisfactory examination in the several professional branches.

Examinations for promotion.

15. Boards of examiners, in deciding on the relative merit and fitness of passed assistant or assistant surgeons exam-

ined for promotion at any one time, will be governed by seniority, unless there are specific reasons for waiving that provision.

16. The compensation of surgeons, passed assistant surgeons, and assistant surgeons will be fixed by the Secretary of the Treasury, at a uniform annual rate for each grade. *Compensation of medical officers.*

17. Medical officers serving at United States marine hospitals shall, when practicable, receive quarters, fuel, and lights. *Perquisites of medical officers.*

18. Medical officers will be required to procure the prescribed uniform of their rank, and shall wear the same while on duty. *Prescribed uniform to be worn.*

19. The full-dress uniform is to be worn while serving on examining boards, on weekly inspection duty, and on all special occasions. The undress uniform is to be worn at all other times.

20. Acting assistant surgeons of the Marine-Hospital Service will be appointed by the Secretary of the Treasury, upon the recommendation of the Supervising Surgeon-General. *Acting assistant surgeons.*

21. Candidates for appointment as acting assistant surgeons must be competent physicians and surgeons of good moral and professional standing. *Qualifications.*

22. Acting assistant surgeons of the Marine-Hospital Service will be required to perform the same official duties as the regular medical officers of that Service, with the exception that they will not issue certificates of service, or hospital-permits, nor keep the register of permits, except where so ordered by the Supervising Surgeon-General, and will not be subject to change of station unless with their consent, and will not be detailed on examining boards. *Duties.*

23. A medical officer will not be allowed to remain at any one station for a longer period than four years, unless specially authorized by the Department. *Length of service at stations.*

### COMPENSATION.

24. The compensation of acting assistant surgeons will be fixed by the Secretary of the Treasury at annual rates, and according to the extent and importance of the service at their respective stations. *Pay of acting assistant surgeons.*

25. Medical officers, acting assistant surgeons, and hospital-stewards of the Marine-Hospital Service shall not receive compensation except while on duty, sick, under orders, or on authorized leave. *When officers to receive pay.*

Compensation of officers paid monthly.

26. The compensation of medical officers and acting assistant surgeons in the Marine-Hospital Service shall be paid at the close of each month, with such exceptions only as are provided for in these regulations.

Pay-rolls to conform to official salary-table.

27. In preparing the pay-rolls of the Service, the Government salary-tables furnished by the Treasury Department will be adhered to in all cases where the compensation is at an annual rate.

Forms 1939, 1940.

Salary to begin from oath of office.

28. On the first payment after appointment or promotion, the medical officer or acting assistant surgeon will be paid from the date of his oath of office.

## LEAVES OF ABSENCE.

Medical officers and others not to leave station without authority.

29. Medical officers, acting assistant surgeons, and stewards shall not absent themselves from their respective posts, unless granted leave of absence by the Secretary of the Treasury, except as hereinafter provided.

Applications for leave of absence.

30. Applications for leave of absence, made by medical officers and acting assistant surgeons of the Marine-Hospital Service, will be addressed to the Supervising Surgeon-General.

Leave of absence not to exceed thirty days.

31. Leaves of absence shall not exceed thirty days in each calendar year, except in case of sickness, and leaves of absence in excess of thirty days, if granted for other cause, shall be without pay.

U. S. Statutes at Large, v. 22, p. 564, c. 128, s. 5.

Temporary leave may be granted by surgeon in charge.

32. Leave of absence for one week, or less, may be granted by the surgeon in charge of a relief station to any subordinate officer or employé, such leave of absence to be noted on the monthly pay-roll. The sum total of such leave shall not exceed thirty days in any calendar year.

Officers on leave to keep Surgeon-General informed of address.

33. Medical officers and acting assistant surgeons, when absent on leave authorized by the Department, will inform the Supervising Surgeon-General of changes in their post-office address as they may occur.

## CHANGES OF STATION, ETC.

Transfers of station.

34. Medical officers, acting assistant surgeons, hospital-stewards, and employés, when transferred from one station to another, and when on special duty, will keep the Supervising Surgeon-General informed of their movements. They will report promptly the date of their departure from a station, and the date of their arrival at the point of destination.

35. Medical officers, acting assistant surgeons, hospital-stewards, and other employés will be entitled to their actual and necessary travelling expenses while travelling under official orders. Travelling expenses allowed.

36. Medical officers and others will advance their own travelling expenses, except over land-grant lines of railroad, when transportation orders over such lines will be issued by the Department.* Travelling expenses advanced by officers.

37. Medical officers and others, upon completing the duty specified in their official orders, will forward to the Supervising Surgeon-General, for reimbursement, an account of the travelling expenses, arranged in chronological order, with an affidavit that the account is correct. Reimbursement of travelling expenses.

38. Receipts will be taken in all cases, where it is practicable to obtain them, and will accompany the account as sub-vouchers. No charge will be allowed for hotel-bills when the detention is unnecessary for the performance of the duties for which travel is required. Sub-vouchers to be taken.

39. The actual and necessary travelling expenses allowed medical officers, acting assistant surgeons, and hospital stewards shall embrace the following items of expenditure: Actual fares on railroads, steamboats, or other conveyances, by the shortest practicable route. Street-car, omnibus, or transfer-coach fare to and from depots and hotels and other places necessarily visited, and, when there are no such conveyances, moderate and necessary hack-fare, and reasonable fees to porters and expressmen. Sleeping-car fare, with one double-berth for each person, or customary state-room accommodation on steamboats and other vessels. One seat in parlor-car, and lodgings and actual board at a rate not greater than $5 per day. Schedule of travelling expenses allowed.

40. Medical officers and others, when transferred from one station to another, shall be entitled to the actual and necessary cost of board and lodging for three days from the date of arrival at the last station, at a rate not greater than $5 each day. Allowance for hotel expenses.

41. The allowance of baggage to officers, in changing stations, will be, for surgeons, two thousand pounds; passed assistant surgeons, fifteen hundred pounds; assistant surgeons, twelve hundred pounds; and for hospital-stewards, five hundred pounds. In all cases this allowance shall be Allowance for baggage.

---

*The lines referred to in paragraph 36 are the following:
Central Pacific, Kansas Pacific, Union Pacific, Central Branch, U. P., Western Pacific, Sioux City and Pacific, their branches and leased lines.

for baggage actually owned by the officer, and sent as freight, and the receipted freight-bill will accompany the travelling-expense account as a voucher. Bills for express-charges will not be allowed unless previously authorized.

## HOSPITAL-STEWARDS.

**Appointment of hospital-stewards.** 42. Hospital-stewards will be appointed to the general service by the Secretary of the Treasury, upon the recommendation of a medical officer and the approval of the Supervising Surgeon-General.

**Qualifications.** 43. Candidates for appointment as hospital-stewards must present evidence of good moral character, and must pass a satisfactory examination before a medical officer of the Marine-Hospital Service as to their qualifications in pharmacy and book-keeping.

**Compensation.** 44. The compensation of hospital-stewards shall be fixed by the Secretary of the Treasury at annual rates, and on the first payment after appointment or promotion they will be paid from the date of oath.

**Classes.** 45. Hospital-stewards shall be divided into three classes, first, second, and third, and original appointments shall be to the third class.

**Promotions.** 46. Promotions according to seniority or merit, upon recommendation of the medical officers under whom they have served, will be made, after one year's service, from the lower to the next grade.

**Suspension for cause.** 47. Hospital-stewards may be suspended by the surgeon in charge for dishonesty, imcompetency, insubordination, neglect of duty, or any other sufficient cause; but the facts shall in every such case be immediately reported to the Department, through the Supervising Surgeon-General, for approval.

**Perquisites.** 48. Hospital-stewards, when on duty in United States marine hospitals, shall be entitled to quarters, subsistence, fuel, and lights.

**Uniform to be worn.** 49. Hospital-stewards will be required to procure the prescribed uniform of their rank, and shall wear the same while on duty.

**Hospital-stewards to give bond.**
**Form 1902.** 50. Hospital-stewards on duty in United States marine hospitals who are charged, under the direction of the surgeon in charge, with the care and preservation of property, shall give a good and sufficient bond, in the penal sum of one thousand dollars, for the faithful performance of their duties.

51. The general duties of a hospital-steward shall be, General duties. unless otherwise directed by the medical officer in charge, to oversee the duties of the hospital attendants and that they are properly performing their respective work, to report dereliction of duty among the employés to the surgeon in charge. to supervise the cleansing of wards and out-buildings, and to preserve order in and about the buildings and grounds.

52. It shall be the special duty of hospital-stewards to Special duties. procure the subsistence and other supplies as directed by the surgeon in charge, to keep a record. by weight or measure, of all the stores received, and also of the stores issued each day to the cook or patients; to compound and dispense such medicines as may be prescribed by the medical officer in charge. and to visit the wards daily in company with the medical officer at sick-call to receive his orders, unless otherwise ordered.

53. Hospital-stewards shall keep such accounts and rec- Accounts kept by stewards. ords pertaining to the management of the Service as they may be directed to do by the surgeon in charge, and, unless otherwise ordered at the discretion of the medical officer in charge, shall keep the following accounts and books :

Property return.
Monthly report of subsistence.
Inventory of patients' effects.
Record of subsistence and other supplies.
Inventory of furniture.
Inventory of medical supplies.
Record of liquors consumed.
Record of letters and papers sent.
Record of letters and papers received.

### HOSPITAL ATTENDANTS.

54. At marine hospitals attendants will be authorized as Appointment. the necessities of the Service require. and will be nominated by the surgeon in charge of the station, subject to the approval of the Department.

55. When submitting nominations for appointment to Information concerning, to subordinate positions, medical officers will forward to the be reported in nomination. Surgeon-General the following information : Name, age, place of birth of nominee, the State from whence appointed and record of service, if any, in the Army or Navy during the war of the rebellion.

Preference of persons disabled in military or naval service.

R. S., (1878,) Title xix, s. 1754; 3 Mar., 1865. Res. No. 27, s. 1, v. 13, p. 71.

56. Persons honorably discharged from the military or naval service by reason of disability resulting from wounds or sickness incurred in the line of duty, shall be preferred for appointment, provided they are found to possess the capacity necessary for the proper discharge of the duties of hospital attendants.

Changes of hospital attendants.

57. Medical officers in charge of relief-stations will report immediately any changes made in the *personnel* of the hospital attendants; stating in each case the full name and duties of the person whose employment has been terminated, and the reasons for the change made.

To be known as hospital attendants.

58. Subordinate employés and laborers in United States marine hospitals shall be known and styled as hospital attendants, and will be borne on the roll as such. They shall be required to perform whatever duties may be assigned to them by the medical officer in charge, or the hospital steward acting under his orders.

Uniform to be worn.

59. Hospital attendants are required to provide themselves with the prescribed uniform of their grade and to wear the same on duty and during temporary leave of absence.

Number allowed.

60. The number of hospital attendants for a hospital having a daily average of not less than twenty patients will be seven, to be detailed as follows, viz : One as nurse ; one as watchman, who must be competent to act as night-nurse ; one as ambulance-driver and gardener ; one as cook ; one as laundress, and two for general service in the dining-rooms and about the building and grounds.

Additional attendants allowed.

61. The basis for additional employés will be as follows, viz : One assistant nurse for every twenty patients in addition to the first twenty ; one assistant cook, and one assistant laundress when the number of patients exceeds forty.

Duties.

62. Hospital attendants after performing their prescribed daily duties will report to the hospital-steward for further orders.

Not to leave grounds without permission.

63. Hospital attendants will not leave the hospital grounds without permission from the medical officer or hospital-steward.

Not to perform household work for officers.

64. Hospital attendants will not be required or allowed to perform any household or laundry work for the benefit of a medical officer of the Service or his family.

65. Hospital attendants may be granted leave of absence, not exceeding seven days, by the medical officer in charge, but such leave of absence is to be noted on the pay-roll for the month or months in which the attendant was absent. *Leave of absence.*

66. The medical officer in charge of a station will be held responsible for the maintenance of discipline among the employés, and the proper performance of the duties allotted to them ; and when any employé wilfully disobeys official orders, or for other good cause, such employé may be summarily dismissed by the surgeon in charge, who will report the facts to the Department for approval. *Dismissal for cause.*

67. Hospital attendants when on duty at a marine hospital shall be entitled to quarters, fuel, light, subsistence, and washing. *Perquisites.*

2 R R

# DISCIPLINE.

# DISCIPLINE.

68. Medical officers and acting assistant surgeons of the Marine-Hospital Service are not subject to any official orders except those emanating from superior officers of that Service, or from the Secretary or Assistant Secretaries of the Treasury. Orders to be obeyed from superiors.

69. When more than one medical officer is assigned to duty at a station, the senior officer shall be in charge, and shall be held accountable to the Department for the administration of the Service. Senior officer to have charge of station.

70. The medical officer in charge of a station shall have authority over all officers and employés of that station and, is empowered to enforce such orders as he may deem necessary for the proper management and discipline of the hospital, subject to the approval of the Supervising Surgeon-General. Officer in charge to have authority over subordinates.

71. Medical officers, and subordinates are required to treat their official superiors with proper respect, and to obey all orders of such superior officers not in conflict with the regulations. Subordinate officers to be respectful and obedient.

72. No officer or employé attached to the Marine-Hospital Service will be permitted to oppress or maltreat any person under his command, or in the Service, nor to abuse applicants for relief, or patients under their care. Maltreatment of subordinates or patients not permitted.

73. When the medical officer in charge of a station is temporarily absent, the officer next below him in rank will perform such ordinary duties of his superior officer as cannot, without injury to the Service, be delayed until his return. In absence of senior officer, next ranking officer to assume duties.

74. When two or more medical officers are serving at the same station, the junior officers will forward official communications through the surgeon in charge, except in his absence, when the next ranking officer will act in his stead. The papers and communications of acting assistant surgeons will be forwarded through the collectors of customs at their respective stations, unless otherwise ordered. Any remarks or recommendations of customs officers in Official letters to be sent through senior officer.

reference to official communications of acting assistant surgeons will be indorsed on said communications.

Use of intoxicating beverages to excess.

75. No person habitually using intoxicating beverages to excess shall be appointed to or retained in any office, appointment, or employment in the Marine-Hospital Service.

U. S. Statutes at Large, v. 22, p. 406, c. 31, s. 8.

# GENERAL DUTIES OF MEDICAL OFFICERS.

# GENERAL DUTIES OF MEDICAL OFFICERS.

76. The duties of officers of the medical corps are professional, sanitary, and executive.

General duties.

77. The professional duties of a medical officer are to examine all applicants for relief, to prescribe and furnish medicine or hospital treatment as may be required, and to make physical examinations of seamen of the several Government services and merchant marine, under such regulations as shall hereinafter appear.

Professional duties.

78. The sanitary duties of a medical officer are to obey the local health laws in force at their respective stations, to execute or aid in executing the restraints of national quarantine laws, when declared to be in force at their respective stations, and to inspect the various hospitals where seamen are treated, under such regulations as shall hereinafter appear.

Sanitary duties.

April 29, 1878, s. 3; 20 Stat., p. 38.

79. The executive duties of a medical officer are to keep all records relating to relief at the station, to preserve the public property in his charge, to act as custodian (ex-officio) of the buildings and grounds, and to supervise all subordinate officers and employés and the administration of the Service at the port, under such regulations as shall hereinafter appear.

Executive duties.

## PROFESSIONAL DUTIES.

80. Medical officers will, upon the application of any United States shipping commissioner, or of the master or owner of any United States vessel engaged in the foreign trade, or of any passenger-steamer engaged in the coasting or inland-navigation trade, examine as to his physical condition any seaman brought to them for that purpose, and will give a certificate (Form 1928) as to his fitness or unfitness for service. They will physically examine, in accordance with existing regulations governing the physical examination of American seamen, any foreign seamen sent them for that purpose by the duly authorized agent of a foreign line or the consul representing the nation to which the vessel belongs. A fee of fifty cents will be charged for such exam-

To examine applicants for relief, and certain other persons as to physical qualifications for enlistment in Government service. (See Appendix.)

Department Circular No. 118, Oct. 17, 1882.

inations. and fees so received will be deposited with the collector of customs in the same manner as donations to the marine-hospital fund. Medical officers will also, upon the application of the proper officers, examine enlisted men and persons desiring to enlist in the Revenue-Marine. Life-Saving. Coast-Survey, and Light-House Services, or to instruct them in the mode of resuscitating persons apparently drowned.

**Examinations to be made at offices.** 81. Medical inspections of seamen, with reference to their fitness for service, will be made only at the respective marine-hospital offices. except at certain stations where the Secretary of the Treasury may authorize such examinations to be made elsewhere in special cases.

**No fee to be charged.** 82. No fee will be charged by any medical officer of the Marine-Hospital Service for the medical inspection of any American seaman or for making a certificate as to his physical condition.

**Color-blindness and visual tests.** 83. When requested by the local inspectors of steamvessels or other proper officers, medical officers and acting assistant surgeons will examine applicants for pilot's license as to color-blindness and general visual capacity, and will give a certificate accordingly.

## SANITARY DUTIES.

**To aid in quarantine restraints.**

**Apr. 29, 1878, s. 3.** 84. It shall be the duty of the medical officers of the Marine-Hospital Service to aid in the enforcement of the national quarantine rules and regulations; but no additional compensation shall be allowed said officers by reason of such service as they may be required to perform under this act, except actual and necessary travelling expenses.

**To comply with local health laws.** 85. Medical officers and acting assistant surgeons will inform themselves fully as to the local health laws, and the regulations based thereon, and in force at their respective ports and stations, and will comply strictly therewith.

**To report presence of epidemics.** 86. Medical officers and acting assistant surgeons will report forthwith to the Supervising Surgeon-General any important event or fact that may come to their knowledge bearing upon the importation, outbreak, or spread of cholera, yellow fever, small-pox, typhus, or other epidemic disease. at or near their respective stations, and will use the telegraph if necessary.

**To vaccinate seamen.** 87. Upon the outbreak of epidemic small-pox at or near a relief-station, medical officers and acting assistant surgeons will vaccinate such seamen as may come to the marine-hospital office for the purpose; and officers are authorized, at all times, to visit vessels to examine and vaccinate crews. Vaccine virus will be furnished by the Department upon requisition.

88. An inspection of the food, ventilation, and any matters directly affecting the welfare of the patients of the Marine-Hospital Service, in all hospitals where such patients may be treated, will be made at least once each week by the proper officer in charge of the service at each relief-station, respectively. *To inspect condition of hospitals.*

89. Surgeons in charge of United States marine hospitals shall inspect the quality of the hospital supplies furnished under contract, and shall reject such as are of inferior quality. *To inspect supplies.*

## EXECUTIVE DUTIES.

90. The medical officer in charge of a relief-station will be held responsible for the proper and economical conduct of the service at said station, and for the care and preservation of all public property in his charge. *Medical officers responsible for property.*

91. Each surgeon, on being promoted to that office, and any other medical officer of the Service when assigned to duty in charge of a United States marine hospital, shall be required to give a good and sufficient bond, in the sum of five thousand dollars, with sureties satisfactory to the Secretary of the Treasury, fully to account for all public property which he may receive. The official bond of officers of the Marine-Hospital Service shall be made out in accordance with the blank form furnished by the Treasury Department for that purpose. *Bonds to be given.*

92. Medical officers and acting assistant surgeons shall keep a true account of all public property received by them. For this purpose a proper return shall be rendered by them on the first day of July and first day of January, each year. *To account for property. Forms 1903, 1904.*

93. When any medical officer or acting assistant surgeon of the Service, accountable for any public property, resigns, is transferred to some other relief-station, or otherwise ceases to have charge of said property, he shall prepare an invoice thereof to the officer relieving him, forwarding the same to the Supervising Surgeon-General, with the appended receipt of the officer who receives the property. *Invoices to be made to successors.*

**Property not to be dropped from returns.** 94. No property will be dropped from the property return without authority from the Department, except subsistence and expendable articles.

**Loss of property.** 95. In case of loss of any non-expendable article, the medical officer or acting assistant surgeon of the Service responsible for the property will report to the Department the facts concerning the loss or destruction thereof, at once, accompanied by an affidavit, sworn to before a notary public or other officer.

**Unserviceable property to be reported.** 96. Medical officers and acting assistant surgeons will forward to the Supervising Surgeon-General on the first days of April and October of each year an inventory of all articles of property, for which they are responsible, which have been broken, worn-out, or otherwise rendered unfit for further use, and all such articles will be retained for inspection.

**Authority for dropping unserviceable property.** 97. The duplicate copy of the aproved inspection report authorizing medical officers to drop from their property return any articles lost, destroyed, or condemned, will be transmitted with the semi-annual property returns to which they refer.

**Unserviceable property to be inspected but once.** 98. Unserviceable property which has once been condemned will not again be submitted for inspection.

**Sale of public property. (See advertisement.)** 99. Property belonging to the Marine-Hospital Service shall not be disposed of at private sale. When authority has been obtained from the Secretary of the Treasury to dispose of such property, it will be sold at public sale. after due notice, either by advertisement or posting in places frequented by the public.

**Final accounts of officers not to be paid until property returns are settled.** 100. The final accounts of medical officers of the Marine Hospital Service will not be paid until their property returns shall have been examined and found to be correct.

## INSPECTIONS OF STATIONS AND PROPERTY.

**Duties of inspectors.** 101. Medical officers, when detailed to inspect relief-stations, shall inform themselves fully as to the conduct of the service and the observance of the Regulations at each port inspected, and shall carefully examine the books. reports. files, correspondence, local hospitals under contract, and the buildings and property for which the officer in charge is responsible, and shall report the condition of the same.

102. When an unfavorable report is made on any subject by an inspecting officer, he will in all cases make a recommendation embodying his opinion as to the remedy.

Unfavorable reports and recommendations.

103. In making reports of inspections of the service at several stations a separate report will be made for each station.

Separate reports for each station.

104. Officers visiting relief-stations under orders for purposes of inspection, will examine the journal, and note therein the general condition of the service at each station as they find it.

Inspections to be entered in journal.

105. Articles of property inspected by medical officers or boards, under instructions from the Department, will be reported upon fully as to their condition, with recommendations for their disposal, (Form 1909.) Such articles as can be repaired or utilized by the Service will not be recommended to be sold or destroyed. Reports of the inspection of unserviceable property will be forwarded to the Supervising Surgeon-General in duplicate.

Recommendation concerning property inspected.

Reports of inspection.

## DUTIES AS CUSTODIANS.

106. Medical officers or acting assistant surgeons will be appointed by the Secretary of the Treasury as *ex-officio* custodians of marine hospitals and buildings of the station of which they are in charge, without extra compensation, and they will have control and supervision of the buildings so intrusted to them.

Medical officers designated as custodians of marine hospitals.

Customs Regulations, 1884, pt. vii, c. 6, art. 1501.

107. They will cause the halls, stairs, vestibules, passageways, and rooms to be kept clean at all times, and will take such measures as may be necessary to prevent nuisances about the building and grounds. The wards and quarters of hospital attendants must be in good order before 11 o'clock, A. M., of each day.

Custodians to cause buildings and grounds to be kept in order.

Ibid., art. 1502.

108. They will not allow any of the rooms in the building to be used for other than official purposes, except those assigned as quarters, and will make no assignment of rooms without authority from the Secretary of the Treasury.

Rooms in building to be used for official purpose only.

Ibid., art. 1511.

109. Any necessity for repairs or alterations of the building, of the furniture or fixtures therein, of the approaches to the building, or of the fences enclosing the grounds, will be promptly reported by them to the Secretary of the Treasury, together with an estimate of the cost of making the same, and their opinion in regard thereto.

Necessity for repairs, &c., to be reported.

Ibid., art. 1505.

Unauthorized expenditures are illegal.

*Ibid.,* art. 1507.

110. Expenditures for repairs, furniture, and other objects, made without previous authority, are in violation of law, and will not be permitted, and application must be made to the Secretary of the Treasury, for any improvement or alteration of the building, or articles of furniture that may be required therein.

Emergency expenditures will be allowed.

*Ibid.,* art. 1506.

111. Custodians will not incur expenditures for repairs, alterations, furniture, and other necessaries without the previous written authority of the Department, except in case of sudden break or defect in plumbing, gas-fixtures, or heating apparatus, or leak in the roof of the building, when they will cause the necessary repairs to be made, and immediately report the same to the Department.

If authorized expenditure is insufficient.

*Ibid.,* art. 1506.

112. When an amount authorized for any specific purpose proves insufficient, authority must be obtained for any additional expense before submitting vouchers for payment.

Custodians to make estimates of expenditures.

*Ibid.,* art. 1508.

113. Custodians will prepare and transmit, for payment, vouchers for all expenditures authorized, charging them to the appropriation specified in the letter authorizing the expenditure, which must also be referred to by date.

Estimates to be submitted in detail, &c.

*Ibid.,* art. 1509.

114. Estimates of expense payable from the several appropriations for public buildings should be submitted in detail, and special articles of furniture should be accompanied by a sketch.

Requisitions not oftener than once a month.

*Ibid.,* art. 1511. Synopsis of Decisions, No. 3296.

115. Custodians will not make requisitions for articles needed in public buildings under their charge oftener than once a month.

Proposals for fuel.

*Ibid.,* art. 1509.

116. Proposals for supplying fuel should be made to include all expense incidental to weighing, delivering, and stowing.

Notices, except for public business, not to be posted.

*Ibid.,* art. 1504.

117. Advertisements or public notices, except such as relate to public business, must not be posted on the walls or in the corridors or public lobbies of the building.

Diagrams of rooms and occupation of same to be forwarded annually.

118. Custodians will forward annually on the 30th of June to the Supervising Architect, Treasury Department, rough diagrams of the different floors of the buildings under their charge, showing by whom the several rooms are occupied.

119. Custodians will make application to renew leases of buildings at least sixty days before the expiration of existing leases, giving a list of all buildings and rooms rented at their station, the purposes and periods for which they are leased, the annual rent paid, that the premises are suitable for the purpose designed, that the rent charged is as low as suitable premises can be obtained, and that the lessor can give a valid lease.

Applications for leases and renewals.

Synopsis of Decisions, No. 3947.
Ibid., art. 1510.

120. Should it be necessary to keep fires burning all night, in order to preserve a proper temperature during the winter season, the custodians will, at the proper time, report such fact to the Secretary of the Treasury, together with their recommendations as to the additional force of firemen which may be required for the purpose.

Heating buildings at night.

Ibid., art. 1503.

121. Each marine hospital shall be entitled to two national ensigns, one of which shall be hoisted from a staff erected over or near the executive building of the hospital each day from 9 A. M. to sunset, except during stormy weather.

Flags.

122. Surgeons in charge of marine hospitals will use every possible precaution to guard against danger of destruction of the buildings and other property by fire. Fire-buckets are to be kept filled with water, ready for use, and must not be removed from their proper places, or used for any other purpose than extinguishing fire, and the hospital attendants will, from time to time, be instructed and drilled by the hospital-steward, under the direction of the surgeon in charge, in the proper use of the fire-extinguishing apparatus that may be provided.

Precautions against fire.

123. Once a week, and oftener if necessary, the surgeon in charge of any United States marine hospital shall make a thorough inspection of all wards, rooms, offices, water-closets, &c., in the building, including the linen-room, subsistence store-room, dispensary, &c., and at least once in each month this inspection shall extend to the out-buildings and grounds.

Inspection of buildings and grounds.

124. Persons or corporations demanding payments in advance for gas, water, or other service, or supplies for the public use, will be notified that, under the restrictive provisions of the statutes, no account can be paid except for service, &c., rendered at the date of presentation of such account.

Advance payment of bills.

# RELIEF-STATIONS.

# RELIEF-STATIONS.

—

125. A relief-station of the Marine-Hospital Service is a Definition. port situated on any navigable water of the United States where an officer of the customs or Marine-Hospital Service is on duty.

126. All relief-stations where the service is under the Classes. charge of a medical officer of the Marine-Hospital Service shall be known as relief-stations of Class 1. Relief-stations where specific arrangements have been made for the care and treatment of sick or disabled seamen at rates fixed by the Treasury Department, but where collectors of customs, on account of the absence of a medical officer of the Service, are authorized and required to issue permits, and to supervise the relief furnished, shall be known as relief-stations of Class 2. All other ports where there are officers of the customs revenue, but where, on account of the infrequency of applications for relief, the absence of any hospital, or from other causes, sick or disabled seamen are cared for only in cases of emergency, shall be known as relief-stations of Class 3.

127. The relief-stations of the Marine-Hospital Service Districts. are grouped into eight districts, as follows: The District of the North Atlantic, the District of the Middle Atlantic, the District of the South Atlantic, the District of the Gulf. the District of the Ohio, the District of the Mississippi. the District of the Great Lakes, and the District of the Pacific.

128. The district of the North Atlantic embraces the fol- North Atlantic. lowing-named relief-stations, viz: Bangor, Maine; Barnstable, Mass.; Bath, Maine; Belfast, Maine; Boston, Mass.; Bristol, R. I.; Burlington, Vt.; Castine, Maine; Eastport. Maine; Edgartown, Mass.; Ellsworth, Maine; Fall River, Mass.; Gloucester, Mass.; Hyannis, Mass.; Kennebunk, Maine; Machias, Maine; Marblehead, Mass.; Nantucket, Mass.; New Bedford. Mass.; Newburyport, Mass.; Newport. R. I.; Plattsburg, N. Y.; Plymouth, Mass.; Portland, Maine; Portsmouth, N. H.; Providence, R. I.; Rockland, Maine; Saco, Maine; Salem, Mass.; Vineyard Haven, Mass.; Waldo-

boro'. Maine; Wiscasset, Maine: and York. Maine: together with all other relief-stations situated in the same
customs districts.

Middle Atlan- 129. The district of the Middle Atlantic embraces the
tic. following-named relief-stations, viz: Albany, N. Y.; Bridge-
port. Conn.; Bridgeton. N. J.; Greenport, N. Y.; Lamber-
ton, N. J.; Middletown, Conn.; Newark. N. J.; New Haven,
Conn.: New London, Conn.; New York, N. Y.; Patchogue.
N. Y.; Perth Amboy, N. J.; Philadelphia, Pa.; Sag Harbor.
N. Y.; Somers Point, N. J., Stonington, Conn.; Troy,N. Y.;
Tuckerton, N. J.; and Wilmington, Del.; together with all
other relief-stations situated in the same customs districts.

South Atlan- 130. The district of the South Atlantic embraces the fol-
tic. lowing-named relief-stations. viz: Alexandria, Va.; An-
napolis, Md.; Baltimore, Md.; Beaufort, N. C.; Beaufort.
S. C.; Brunswick, Ga.; Charleston, S. C.; Crisfield, Md.;
Eastville, Va.; Edenton, N. C.; Fernandina, Fla.; George-
town, D. C.; Georgetown, S. C.; Jacksonville, Fla.; New
Berne, N. C.; Norfolk, Va.; Petersburg, Va.; Richmond,
Va.; Saint Augustine, Fla.; Savannah, Ga.; Tappahannock.
Va.; and Wilmington, N. C.; together with all other relief-
stations situated in the same customs districts.

Gulf. 131. The district of the Gulf embraces the following-
named relief-stations or ports, viz: Apalachicola, Fla.;
Brashear, La.; Brownsville, Tex.; Cedar Keys, Fla.;
Corpus Christi, Tex.; El Paso, Tex.; Galveston, Tex.; Key
West, Fla.; Mobile. Ala.; New Orleans, La.; Pensacola,
Fla.; Shieldsboro', Miss.; and Shreveport, La.; together
with subordinate ports.

Ohio. 132. The district of the Ohio embraces the following-
named relief-stations or ports, together with all subordinate
ports, viz: Chattanooga. Tenn.; Cincinnati, Ohio; Evans-
ville, Ind.; Louisville, Ky.; Nashville, Tenn.; Paducah,
Ky.; Parkersburg, W. Va.; Pittsburgh, Pa.; and Wheeling,
W. Va.

Mississippi. 133. The district of the Mississippi embraces the follow-
named relief-stations or ports, together with all subordinate
ports, viz: Bismarck, Dak.; Burlington, Iowa; Cairo, Ill.;
Dubuque, Iowa; Galena, Ill.; La Crosse, Wis.; Memphis,
Tenn.; Natchez, Miss.; Omaha, Nebr.; Pembina, Dak.; Saint
Louis, Mo.; Saint Paul, Minn.; and Vicksburg, Miss.

Great Lakes. 134. The district of the Great Lakes embraces the following-named relief-stations, viz: Buffalo, N. Y.; Cape Vin-

cent, N. Y.; Chicago, Ill.; Cleveland, Ohio.; Detroit, Mich.; Duluth, Minn.; Dunkirk, N. Y.; Erie, Pa.; Escanaba, Mich.; Grand Haven, Mich.; Green Bay, Wis.; Kenosha, Wis.; L'Anse, Mich.; Manitowoc, Wis.; Marquette, Mich.; Milwaukee, Wis.; Muskegon, Mich.; Ogdensburg, N. Y.; Oswego, N. Y.; Racine, Wis.; Rochester, N. Y.; St. Joseph, Mich.; Sandusky, Ohio; Sault Ste. Marie, Mich.; Sheboygan, Wis.; and Toledo, Ohio; together with all other relief-stations situated in the same customs districts.

135 The district of the Pacific embraces the following-named relief-stations, viz: Astoria, Oreg.; Empire City, Oreg.; Portland, Oreg.; Port Townsend, Wash.; San Diego, Cal.; San Francisco, Cal.; and Sitka, Alaska; together with all other relief-stations situated in the same customs districts. *Pacific.*

136. At all relief-stations where the number of patients warrant, a medical officer of the Marine-Hospital Service will be assigned in charge, and, whenever practicable, the patients of the Service will be treated in hospitals maintained exclusively for their benefit. At places where Congress has made no provision for the erection of a marine hospital, or where the number of patients does not warrant the erection of one, buildings or rooms suitable for hospital purposes, or separate wards in State, municipal, or private hospitals, may be leased or rented for the exclusive benefit of the patients of the Service, subject to the approval of the Secretary of the Treasury. *Provisions for relief.*

137. The medical and surgical treatment of the patients of the Marine-Hospital Service will be under the supervision of the medical officers of the Service at all relief-stations where such officers are on duty, and they will be required to take direct professional charge of the patients. *Supervision of relief at large ports.*

138. At each relief-station of the first class, and whenever practicable, at each relief-station of the second class where an acting assistant surgeon of the Marine-Hospital Service is on duty, there shall be a marine-hospital office, where applicants for relief shall be received and examined, and their applications acted upon. *Supervision of relief at small ports.*

139. The marine-hospital dispensary shall be located at the custom-house whenever practicable, and suitable office-room for that purpose will be set apart by the custodian of the custom-house building, subject to the approval of the Secretary of the Treasury. *Offices and dispensaries.*

Assignment
of officers to
stations.

140. At each United States marine hospital a medical officer will be assigned to duty as surgeon in charge; and, whenever necessary, additional medical officers will be assigned as assistants, in which event one officer shall be on duty in the marine-hospital office during business hours.

# BENEFICIARIES OF THE SERVICE,

AND

## THE MANNER IN WHICH RELIEF IS EXTENDED TO THEM.

141. The persons entitled to the benefits of the Marine-Hospital Service are those employed on board in the care, preservation, or navigation of any vessel. or in the service, on board, of those engaged in such care. preservation. or navigation, excepting persons employed in or connected with the navigation. management. or use of canal-boats engaged in the coasting trade.

*List of persons entitled to relief.*

*R. S., s. 4804.*
*Department Circular No. 23, Feb. 27, 1882.*

142. Seamen taken from wrecked vessels of the United States, if sick or disabled, are entitled to the benefits of the Marine-Hospital Service and will be furnished care and treatment without reference to the length of time for which they have been employed.

*Wrecked seamen entitled.*

143. Destitute American seamen returned to the United States from foreign ports by United States consular officers, if sick or disabled at the time of their arrival in a port of the United States, shall be entitled to the benefits of the Marine-Hospital Service.

*Seamen sent by consular officers entitled.*

144. At relief-stations of the first class, the medical officer of the Service in charge, and at relief-stations of the second or third class. the proper customs officer, acting as the agent of the Marine-Hospital Service. will receive the applications of persons claiming the benefits of the marine-hospital fund for care and treatment while sick or disabled.

*Officers authorized to examine applicants.*

145. A sick or disabled seaman, in order to obtain the benefits of the Marine-Hospital Service, must apply to a medical officer of that Service, or, in the absence of such officer, then to the proper customs officer acting as the agent of the Marine-Hospital Service, and must furnish satisfactory evidence that he is entitled to relief under the Regulations.

*Seamen must make application for relief.*

146. Masters' certificates and discharge-papers from United States shipping commissioners, properly made out and signed, showing that the applicant has been employed on a documented vessel or vessels of the United States for at least sixty days immediately preceding his application for relief, shall, in general, be held to constitute the "satisfactory evidence" required.

*Evidence to be presented by applicant.*

*Form 1914.*

Certificates from owners or agents as evidence.

147. The certificate of the owner or accredited commercial agent of a vessel as to the facts of the employment of any seaman on said vessel may be accepted as evidence in lieu of the master's certificate in cases where the latter is not procurable.

Masters enjoined to furnish certificate of service.

148. Masters of vessels of the United States shall, on demand, furnish any seaman who has been employed on such vessel a certificate (Form 1914) of the length of time said seaman has been so employed, giving the date of his last employment and the date of his discharge. This certificate will be filed in the marine-hospital office, or office of the customs officer, upon application being made for relief, whether the relief is furnished or the claim rejected.

Masters refusing to give certificate.

149. In case the master of any vessel shall fail or refuse to furnish a master's certificate to any seaman that may have been employed on board said vessel within thirty days preceding the seaman's application for relief, the collector of customs shall cause said master, if he be in port, to appear at the marine-hospital office and produce the ship's books.

Seamen to sign certificate.

150. Any seaman who is able to write will be expected to sign his name upon the face of the master's certificate issued to him before said certificate is signed by the master of the vessel.

Requirements as to service.

151. During the season when navigation is open at any port, seamen at that port are not entitled to relief from the Marine-Hospital Service, who, from any cause other than disease or injury, have not, within the sixty days immediately preceding the application for relief, been employed on any American vessel.

Exceptions.

152. When an interval has occurred in the applicant's seafaring service by reason of the closure of navigation, it shall not be considered as excluding him from relief, except the sickness or injury for which he applies for relief be the result of employment on shore, nor shall the phrase "immediately preceding the application" be held as excluding from relief a seaman who has been but a few days away from his vessel, provided he has not abandoned his vocation as seaman for any other employment, nor as excluding a seaman who may have been not more than three months away from his vessel, provided it be satisfactorily shown that such absence was due to sickness.

153. During the season when navigation is closed at any Closure of navigation. port, seamen at that port are not entitled to relief from the Marine-Hospital Service, who, from any cause other than disease or injury, have not been employed on board an American vessel within a period exceeding thirty days prior to the closure of navigation.

154. A seaman who has abandond his vocation for any Forfeiture of claims for abandoning vocation. employment on shore for a period of two months or more, unless debarred from shipping by reason of sickness, disability, or closure of navigation, has thereby forfeited his claim to the benefits of the Marine-Hospital Service.

155. Whenever an applicant for relief presents himself Affidavits may be accepted as evidence. at the marine-hospital office or the custom-house without a master's certificate or shipping commissioner's discharge, and it is impracticable to obtain a master's certificate on account of the absence of the vessel or its master from the port, the affidavit of the applicant as to the facts of his last employment may be accepted as evidence in support of his claim for the benefits of the Marine-Hospital Service. The applicant's affidavit may also be accepted as evidence in cases where the period of his last service, as shown by his papers, is less than sixty days.

156. When the period of the seaman's service on last Brief service on last vessel not a bar to relief. vessel is less than two months, his statement as to previous service may be accepted if supported by satisfactory evidence.

157. In cases of doubt, reasonable effort will be made to Evidence to be verified in case of doubt. verify the genuineness of master's certificates and shipping commissioner's discharges, and of the signatures to the same. Due care will also be exercised to identify the persons presenting master's certificates, to protect the fund against imposition.

158. Memoranda of any collateral evidence and statements Statements of applicants to be indorsed on evidence. of prior service, if certificates are insufficient, submitted by applicants for relief, to establish their right to the benefits of the Marine-Hospital Service, will be indorsed on the master's certificates or other papers offered in evidence and retained on file.

159. When an applicant's claim for relief from the ma- Cases of rejected applicants. rine hospital fund is rejected, the cause or causes for such rejection must be indorsed on the masters' certificates, relief certificates, or other papers in each case, which must then be filed and preserved for future reference.

Certain cases to be submitted to Surgeon-General for decision.

160. In every case where a doubt exists, whether the applicant is entitled to relief under the regulations, the application, accompanied by a statement of the facts, must be immediately referred to the Supervising Surgeon-General for decision; and, when the seaman is in such condition that immediate medical or surgical attendance is necessary, he will be placed under treatment pending the decision, and the action in the case taken by the officer reporting it will be stated in the letter.

Cases admitted pending decision to be numbered in order.

Form 1916.

161. When patients are admitted for treatment pending the decision of the Supervising Surgeon-General, the usual permits will be issued, dated the day on which relief commenced, and numbered consecutively with current permits; and the date of the authorization of the Department will be indorsed on the permit, if relief is authorized.

Expenses for sickness during voyage.

162. The expenses of caring for sick and disabled seamen incurred during a voyage will not be paid from the marine-hospital fund.

Relief only upon certificate of officers.

163. No relief will be furnished at the expense of the marine-hospital fund, except upon the certificate and recommendation of a medical officer of the Marine-Hospital Service, or of a competent physician, showing that the applicant requires medical treatment.

Money not to be paid to seamen for expenses of sickness.

164. In no case will money be paid to a seaman himself, or to his family or friends, out of the marine-hospital fund, as reimbursement for expenses incurred during sickness or disability, whose care and treatment was unauthorized by this Department.

Seamen admitted to quarantine hospitals.

165. The expenses for the care and treatment of seamen entitled to the benefits of the Marine-Hospital Service who, in accordance with the State or municipal health laws and regulations, are taken to quarantine or other hospitals under charge of the local health authorities, will not be paid from the marine-hospital fund.

## DISPENSARY RELIEF.

Cases to be treated at dispensary as out-patients.

166. Sick and disabled seamen entitled under these Regulations to the benefits of the Marine-Hospital Service, whose diseases or injuries are of such a nature that they can properly be relieved by medicine, or dressing, or advice, without admission to hospital, will be treated as out-patients,

and furnished medicines, dressings, surgical appliances, or advice, as the case may require.

167. Seamen will not be furnished relief at their own homes, except by special authority from the Supervising Surgeon-General of the Marine-Hospital Service, and then an allowance for medical attendance and medicines only will be made at rates fixed by the Treasury Department.

*No relief furnished at homes of patients.*

### STATIONS OF THE FIRST CLASS.

168. At relief-stations where medical officers of the Marine-Hospital Service are on duty, the evidence of each out patient's right to relief will be recorded in the register of out-patients, over the initials of the medical officer making the entry, and the certificate and papers in the case filed.

*Records to be made of out-relief.*

### STATIONS OF THE SECOND CLASS.

169. At relief-stations of the second class the relief-certificates (Form 1915) issued for out-patients will be forwarded to the Supervising Surgeon-General as soon as the facts contained therein shall have been recorded in the Register of Out-Patients.

*Relief-certificates to be issued.*

170. When relief of any kind, other than hospital-relief, is furnished, its nature (prescriptions, medicines, surgical appliances, transportation, &c.) will be briefly specified on the relief-certificates, and if hospital-relief (medical treatment in hospital, boarding-house, or at home) be furnished, the number and date of the permit, together with the number of days for which it is issued, will be indorsed on said certificates.

*Character of relief to be reported.*

### STATIONS OF THE THIRD CLASS.

171. Whenever, at a third-class relief-station, an application for relief is presented, the customs officers for the port are authorized and directed to cause out-door or office-relief (medicines, surgical appliances, &c.) to be furnished in accordance with paragraph 166, or to furnish transportation to a relief-station of the first or second class, as the case may be. But when the amount of the appropriation is insufficient, any relief-station of the third class may be discontinued.

*Provisions for relief.*

172. Whenever, in the opinion of the examining physician, the patient is unable to bear transportation without preju-

*Temporary arrangements to be made.*

dice to his recovery, the facts will be at once reported to the Supervising Surgeon-General for instructions, and in case medical or surgical attendance is immediately necessary, the customs officer will, pending action upon the case, provide it if possible, at reasonable and just rates. The customs officer will in such cases employ a competent physician to take professional charge of the patient, and will arrange for suitable quarters, nursing, and diet for the patient, and the arrangements made by him will be reported, together with the rates of charges therefor.

**Unreasonable charges disallowed.** 173. Unreasonable charges for relief furnished in emergency cases will not be allowed by the Department.

**Reason for relief to be given.** 174. At relief-stations of the third class, where delay in preparing and signing the relief-certificates is unavoidable, the symptoms on which the physician's recommendation is based must be given, should he be unable to form any diagnosis.

**Foreign seamen *et al.* not treated.** 175. Foreign seamen or employés of the various Government services will not be treated at stations of the third class.

**Allowance for examinations.** 176. One dollar will be allowed physicians, not medical officers or acting assistant surgeons of the Marine-Hospital Service, for the medical examination of each out-patient who is referred by a customs officer for such examination, whether accompanied by a prescription or not, unless otherwise previously directed by the Department, (by the terms of special agreements or contracts.) This allowance will be made each time it is necessary to send the patient to the physician for further advice; and in cases where an outpatient is relieved more than once, by the direction of the collector of customs, a written request will be made to the physician to that effect, which written request will be attached to the bill of the physician as a sub-voucher.

**Extra compensation for hospital treatment.** 177. No separate compensation or allowance will be made for the medical examination and certificate made by physicians in cases where the applicants examined are placed under hospital treatment or its equivalent at the relief-station where the examination is made, except when treated in hospital by another physician.

## HOSPITAL-RELIEF.

178. A sick or disabled seaman entitled to the benefits of the Marine-Hospital Service shall be admitted to hospital only in cases where the gravity of the disease or injury from which he suffers is such as to require hospital treatment in the opinion of a medical officer or acting assistant surgeon of the Service, or of a reputable physician designated by the Department to act at a place where no medical officer is stationed.

*Cases for hospital treatment.*

### STATIONS OF THE FIRST CLASS.

179. At relief-stations where United States marine hospitals are located, the bed-ticket will be prepared at the marine-hospital office, and given to the patient, and the patient will be admitted on presentation of said bed-ticket, enclosed in a sealed envelope.

*Bed-tickets to be issued.*

*Form 1917.*

180. The bed-ticket, before being delivered to the applicant for relief, must be enclosed in an envelope, sealed, and addressed to the medical officer or other person authorized to receive the patient. The seaman should at the same time be informed that unless presented on the day it is issued the ticket will be forfeited.

*To be valid only for day of issue.*

181. Bed-tickets will be numbered consecutively, in annual series, commencing with the unit on the 1st of July of each year.

*To be numbered consecutively.*

182. Upon the admission of a patient for treatment, the medical officer in charge, acting as the agent of the Service, shall receive his money and other valuables, and give a receipt therefor, (Form 1950.) Upon the termination of the treatment of the patient, his money and other effects shall be returned to him, and the receipt taken up and filed.

*Receipts for money and valuables of patients to be given.*

183. Whenever, in any case, a patient admitted to hospital for a given disease or injury satisfactorily progresses to convalescence from such disease or injury, but, before being sufficiently recovered to be discharged, contracts or develops some other disease not properly a sequel or complication of the original affection or injury, a new bed-ticket may be issued in such cases, by the surgeon in charge, without referring the case to the Department. In each such case the number of the original permit will be referred to, and the disease or injury for which the patient was first

*Complication of original disease.*

placed under treatment will be stated, together with the
result of the treatment for the same.

Patients
treated ninety
days.

Department
Circular No.
107, Oct. 31, 1881.

184. At the expiration of each quarter, medical officers
will report, by letter, the names of patients that have been
under treatment ninety days, and will make a recommendation relative to each case.

Patients may
perform light
duties.

185. Hospital patients of the Marine-Hospital Service
will not be required to perform any labor, except such light
duties as may be assigned them by a medical officer of the
Service.

Hours for sick-
call.

186. The medical officer in charge of a marine hospital
shall visit all patients in hospital once each day, and oftener
if necessary. The visit shall commence at 8.30 A. M. in
summer, and at 9 A. M. in winter, and the medicines ordered
shall be compounded and delivered to the nurses as soon
as practicable after the termination of the visit.

Hospital re-
lief to be re-
corded.

Form 1945.

187. The officer authorized and directed under these
Regulations to furnish relief will keep a register of all permits issued, for which purpose a blank book will be furnished by the Treasury Department.

STATIONS OF THE SECOND CLASS.

Relief to be
furnished on
recommenda-
tion of physi-
cian.

188. Hospital relief will not be furnished at the expense
of the marine-hospital fund, except upon the certificate
and recommendation of an acting assistant surgeon or of
a competent and reputable physician, showing that the
applicant requires medical treatment.

Relief certifi-
cate to be is-
sued.

189. The relief-certificate, in all cases, will be forwarded
to the Supervising Surgeon-General of the Marine-Hospital
Service as soon as issued, except in cases of rejection, and
as hereinafter provided.

Relief certifi-
cate.

190. The certificate of service contained in the relief-
certificate will be so made out as to show whether or not
the applicant has served as an American seamen for sixty
days immediately preceding his application for relief, and
the dates of commencement and termination of his last
employment as such, together with the name of the vessel
on which he last served.

Permits for
hospital relief.

Form 1916.

191. Customs officers or acting assistant surgeons will
issue permits for the care and treatment of such applicants
as may be found to be entitled to the benefits of the Service and require hospital treatment. The period for which
treatment is authorized by the permit should be based

upon the certificate of the medical officer or attending physician, as given in the relief-certificates in accordance with paragraph 222, but should in no case exceed sixty days.

192. Hospital permits will be numbered consecutively, in annual series, commencing with the unit on the 1st of July of each year. To be numbered consecutively.

193. The hospital permit, before being delivered to the applicant for relief, must be enclosed in an envelope, sealed, and addressed to the medical officer or other person authorized to receive the patient. The seaman should at the same time be informed that unless presented on the day it is issued the permit will be forfeited. *Permits valid only on day of issue.*

194. When, at a second-class station, a seaman entitled to the benefits of the Service makes application for admission to hospital after the custom-house or dispensary is closed for the day, the surgeon in charge of the hospital in which the patients of the Marine-Hospital Service are treated may receive the patient, should the case be urgent, and will then report the fact at the marine-hospital office the following day, and present to the proper officer the master's certificate or other evidence upon which his action was based. In the event of a failure to report on the second day for admission as above, the permit, should it be proper to issue one, will be dated on the day when such report is made. *Applications for relief after office hours.*

195. In no case will a permit be antedated, except as provided in the foregoing paragraph, and only to cover one working-day, exclusive of legal holidays. *Permits may be antedated.*

196. Sick and disabled seamen presenting themselves at any hospital where patients of the Marine-Hospital Service are cared for, with hospital permits dated prior to the day when presented, will not be treated at the expense of the marine-hospital fund, except under such provisions as are prescribed by these regulations. *Relief not to be given on antedated permits.*

197. Continuous relief for periods exceeding sixty days will in no case be granted except by special authority from the Department. *Relief not to exceed sixty days.*

198. Whenever in any case hospital treatment is required beyond the period for which the permit was originally issued, application for an extension thereof may be made to the Supervising Surgeon-General one week prior to the expiration of the permit. Application will be made by the *Extension of permits.*

*Form 1918.*

4 R R

attending physician, and forwarded through the officer issuing the original permit. An application for the extension of a hospital permit must set forth the reasons why it is necessary, the actual condition of the patient at the time, and the additional period during which treatment will probably be required, and said application may be repeated in a similar manner if necessary.

**To be referred to on permits.**   199. In all cases where relief is extended by special authority from the Department, the date of the letter authorizing the relief must be indorsed upon the permits in each case.

**Complications of disease for which admitted.**   200. Whenever a patient admitted to hospital for a given disease or injury satisfactorily progresses to convalescence from such disease or injury, but, before being sufficiently recovered to be discharged, contracts or develops some other disease not properly a sequel or complication of the original affection or injury, the facts will be immediately reported by the attending surgeon, through the officer keeping the register of permits, to the Supervising Surgeon-General, and application made by letter for a new permit, a new medical certificate, made out and signed accordingly, to be enclosed with said letter. Should a new permit be issued, the permits will refer to each other, by indorsing on the new the date, number, and diagnosis of the old, and *vice versa.*

**Permit to be forwarded on termination of case.**   201. Upon the termination of treatment of a patient, or the issue of a new permit, the certificate, on the outer middle fold of the permit which has expired, will be filled out and signed by the attending surgeon, and the permit will be immediately forwarded to the Supervising Surgeon-General by the officer keeping the register of permits.

**Diagnosis to be reported in relief certificate.**   202. In all cases where treatment in hospital is required, the diagnosis will, where it is practicable to form one, be stated in the relief-certificate by the medical officer or attending physician, and, should he deem it necessary, the relief-certificates may be retained a day or two for that purpose.

**Exceptions.**   203. An approximate or general diagnosis (such as "heart disease," "renal disease" &c.,) in the medical certificate will be accepted as sufficient in cases where it is found impracticable to make a specific diagnosis ; but in all cases where a specific diagnosis is not given in the medical certificate, it must be afterwards supplied by letter as soon as ascertained, and in every case where an error has been made in a diagnosis certified or reported, the error will be immediately corrected by letter.

## STATIONS OF THE THIRD CLASS.

204. Hospital relief at stations of the third class will not be furnished except in cases of emergency and for a temporary period.

Emergency cases only treated in hospital.

---

## TRANSPORTATION OF SICK SEAMEN.

205. In each case where a sick or disabled seaman is furnished transportation from one station to another for treatment, the relief-certificates should be made out and signed, in duplicate, at the station whence transportation is given. The original will be mailed to the officer in charge of the relief-station where the patient is to be admitted to hospital, and the duplicate will be given to the patient in a sealed envelope.

Details of transportation.

Relief certificates to be furnished on departure.

206. In the absence of specific instructions from the Department as to the transportation routes and the rates to be paid, the current rates charged the public at the time will be allowed for the transportation of seamen. Upon the arrival of the patient he will present the duplicate to the officer authorized to issue permits, and when the permit shall have been issued the original will be indorsed accordingly, and immediately forwarded to the Supervising Surgeon-General the duplicate certificate being retained on file.

Current rates to be charged.

Relief certificates to be presented on arrival.

207. When patients are transferred from one relief-station to another for continued treatment, the medical officer or acting assistant surgeon under whose charge the patient has been treated will send to the receiving officer a clinical history of each case and the results of the treatment adopted.

Clinical history of each case to be furnished.

208. Medical officers and others, when furnishing transportation to seamen, will inform the receiving officer, by mail or telegraph, when the patients may be expected to arrive.

Officers to inform receiving officer of date of probable arrival.

### INSANE SEAMEN.

209. Insane seamen entitled to the benefits of the Marine-Hospital Service may be admitted to the Government hospital for the insane upon the order of the Secretary of the Treasury, and the officers in charge of relief-stations will

Relief for insane seamen.

Mar. 3, 1875, s. 5.

report to the Supervising Surgeon-General any application
for admission to hospital made in behalf of such seamen,
and any cases of insanity that may occur among them,
stating, as far as possible, the name, nativity, and age of
the patient, the date of commencement of insanity, the
form of the disease, its cause, as nearly as may be ascertained, its progress, the present condition of the patient,
the prognosis of the case, the length of time the patient
has been a seaman on American vessels, and the name and
post-office address of his nearest known relative.

### DECEASED SEAMEN.

Relatives to
be notified.

210.  On the death of a patient while under the charge of
the Marine-Hospital Service, notice to receive his effects
shall be given by letter, or otherwise, to his nearest known
relative, and, when said effects are delivered to the latter,
a receipt shall be taken therefor, and filed as in the former
case.

Moneys and
effects to be sub-
ject to call for
three months.

211.  If the moneys and valuable effects of deceased patients are not called for within three months after due notice as above, they will be disposed of as hereinafter provided.

Quarterly re-
ports of same to
be made.

212.  At second and third class stations the collectors of
customs will report quarterly to the Department the name
and description of any and all patients of the Marine-Hospital Service who may have died leaving either money or
valuables, or both, in their hands, respectively, which
shall remain unclaimed after three months.

Burial ex-
penses.

213.  The necessary expenses of a plain burial for deceased
patients of the Service will be paid, but no part of the expenses of the burial of any deceased seaman will be paid for
at the expense of the marine-hospital fund unless said seaman was at the time of his death a patient of the Service.

### FOREIGN SEAMEN AND EMPLOYÈS OF GOVERNMENT SER-
### VICES.

Foreign sea-
men may be
treated.

Sec. 6, act Mar.
3, 1875; 18 Stat.,
485.

214.  The accommodations provided for the care and treatment of the patients of the Marine-Hospital Service are also
available to foreign seamen only at relief-stations where
medical officers or acting assistant surgeons are on duty,
upon the application of the consular officers of their respective nationalities, or upon the application of the masters
of the vessels upon which said seamen serve, provided satis-

factory security is given for the payment of the expenses of such care and treatment at rates fixed by the Secretary of the Treasury; and when treatment is furnished a foreign seamen, the fact will be immediately reported to the Supervising Surgeon-General, in the manner provided in foregoing paragraphs.

215. Seamen employed on vessels of the Navy, vessels of the Coast Survey, Light-House Service, Engineer Corps of the Army, and Mississippi River Commission may be admitted for care and treatment as patients of the Marine-Hospital Service only upon the written request of their respective commanding officers, all such admissions to be immediately reported to the Supervising Surgeon-General by medical officers and acting assistant surgeons, on daily reports or relief certificates. The request in each case should be attached to the bill. *Seamen of various Government services may be admitted.*

216. Medical officers and acting assistant surgeons will transmit with the report of admission the requests made by the proper officers for the admission of seamen of the Light-House Service. *Requests for treatment from certain seamen.*

217. The rate of charge to be made for the care and treatment by the Marine-Hospital Service of seamen of the above-named classes will be fixed by the Department at the beginning of each fiscal year, and will be announced to officers and others in the annual circular containing the contracts for care of seamen. *Charges.*

218. A bill, in duplicate, must be made out, by the medical officer or acting assistant surgeon of the Marine-Hospital Service, for the care of each foreign seaman treated by the Service, said bill to be made out upon the termination of treatment in each case, or on the last day of each quarter, if the treatment extends beyond the close of the regular quarter. One copy of this bill shall be delivered to the collector of customs, who shall at once collect the amount thereof; the other copy shall be forwarded by the medical officer or acting assistant surgeon direct to the Supervising Surgeon-General. *Bills for care and treatment.*

219. Customs officers acting as agents of the Marine-Hospital Service will collect all bills for the care and treatment of foreign seamen by the Marine-Hospital Service upon the termination of treatment in each case, and will render monthly accounts for all moneys collected on account of the care of foreign seamen, said accounts to be accom- *Monthly accounts to be rendered.*

panied by abstracts giving the name and nationality of the patient, date of admission and date of discharge, period of treatment. and amount collected in each case.

Coast and Geodetic Survey.

Department Circular No. 9, Feb. 11, 1881.

220. Bills for the care and treatment of sick and disabled persons attached to vessels of the Coast and Geodetic Survey and Mississippi River Commission, admitted to hospital under the provisions of paragraph 215 of the Regulations governing the Marine-Hospital Service, will be certified by the medical officer in duplicate. one copy delivered to the collector of customs and the other forwarded to this office.

221. Collectors of customs will notify the commanding officer of the vessel. upon whose request the seaman was admitted, of the amount of the bill, and when paid will render their receipt. The money will be deposited as a repayment to the marine-hospital fund, in the manner provided for moneys received for the care of foreign seamen.

# HOSPITAL SUBSISTENCE.

# HOSPITAL SUBSISTENCE.

222. Subsistence, groceries, laundry supplies, and forage Subsistence.
shall be obtained for the United States marine hospitals,
whenever practicable, by contract, after advertisement,
said contracts to be executed by the surgeon in charge in
behalf of the United States.

223. On the first day of May of each year the surgeon Estimates for subsistence.
in charge of each United States marine hospital will for-
ward to the Supervising Surgeon-General an estimate, in Form 1910.
duplicate, of the quantities of subsistence and other supplies required for consumption during the next ensuing
fiscal year.

224. The ordinary articles and quantities of subsistence Subsistence allowed stations.
supplies for ten thousand full rations shall not exceed
eight thousand pounds of meat, fresh and salt; ten thousand pounds of vegetables; ten thousand pounds of breadstuffs and other prepared farinaceous food; one hundred
pounds of tea; three hundred pounds of coffee; fifteen
hundred pounds of sugar; twenty-five gallons of molasses
or syrup; seven hundred gallons of milk; one thousand
pounds of butter; two hundred dozen of eggs; three hundred pounds of lard; fifteen hundred pounds of fresh and
dry fruit; five hundred pounds of salt; twenty-five pounds
of pepper; twenty-five gallons of vinegar; twenty-five gallons of pickles.

225. Upon the approval of the estimate for annual sup- Approved schedules to be furnished dealers.
plies, advertisements for proposals will be published in
accordance with the directions of the Department, and,
upon request, schedules will be furnished dealers in the
articles enumerated, for the purpose of obtaining their proposals.

226. In making schedules of articles on which proposals Schedules to be made specific.
to furnish the supplies may be based, each article must be
fully specified, describing, so far as possible, its kind, brand, Form 1911.
and quality. The exact weight or volume must be given,
in order that there may be no doubt as to what the bidder,
whose proposals are accepted will be required to furnish.

Separate schedules to be made.

227. The surgeon in charge will make separate schedules in accordance with the approved estimate for each of the different classes of articles, namely. for meats, vegetables, breadstuffs. groceries. forage. and ice. These schedules will be furnished in duplicate to all persons who may call for them for the purpose of submitting bids.

Changes in schedules may be made.

228. If more advantageous to the service at particular ports to separate certain articles from any of the groups referrd to. in order to obtain separate proposals from dealers therein. the schedule will be made out accordingly.

Bids from responsible dealers desired.

229. Surgeons in charge of marine hospitals will make reasonable effort to induce the largest and most responsible dealers at the station to submit proposals to furnish subsistence and other supplies.

Three bids required in each class.

230. Proposals from at least three dealers in the respective articles will be required, if obtainable, for each class of supplies.

Instructions for dealers.

Department Circular No. 20, Mar. 14, 1883.

231. Dealers will be instructed that the proposals must be delivered in duplicate, and in sealed envelopes, marked "Proposals for hospital supplies," over the signature of the firm. Sufficient sureties will be required with each proposal.

Opening of proposals.

232. The proposals received will be opened at the time specified in the advertisement, by the surgeon in charge of the marine hospital. in the presence of such bidders as may present themselves.

Samples to be submitted.

233. Samples will be required to be submitted to the surgeon in charge by the several bidders as far as practicable, and the quality of the samples submitted, as well as the prices, will govern the recommendations of the medical officer as to the acceptance of any bid.

Comparative schedule to be made.

234. A comparative schedule of all the proposals received will be prepared and transmitted to the Supervising Surgeon-General, together with the proposals, in duplicate. accompanied by a letter of transmittal, giving the recommendation of the surgeon in charge as to the relative merits of each proposal.

Contracts.

Form 1912.

235. Upon receipt of instructions from the Department as to the proposals accepted, surgeons in charge of the United States marine hospitals will enter into contract with the bidders whose proposals have been accepted, the contracts to be made out in quadruplicate, upon the blank form fur-

nished by the Department for that purpose, and will then be transmitted to the Supervising Surgeon-General.

236. Agreements and contracts made on account of the Marine-Hospital Service, required to be made in legal form, with bonds and sureties, will be certified by the proper customs officers, respectively, as to the sufficiency of the sureties given. How made and certified.

237. The contract may be signed in the firm-name, without seals, but the bond accompanying the contract must be signed by the individual members of the firm and their sureties, and each signature to the bond must have seals attached. When a person signs a contract for a company, a power of attorney or other written evidence that he is authorized to act for the company must accompany the contract. Legal requirements of signing.

238. Contracts or agreements made or entered into by medical officers of the Marine-Hospital Service for work, labor, or material, or supplies of any kind, will not be binding until they shall have been approved by the Secretary of the Treasury, or written authority obtained from him to enter into such contract or agreement. Approval of Department required.

239. Contracts for subsistence and other hospital supplies will be made for one year, commencing on the first day of July of each year, and ending on the 30th of June following. Period of contracts.

240. Medical officers on duty in United States marine hospitals shall have the privilege of purchasing subsistence supplies, at the contract rates, from contractors furnishing said hospitals, and a clause to that effect may be included in each contract. Medical officers may have benefit of contracts.

241. Should there be reason to suspect collusion among dealers to obtain more than a fair market price for articles required to be purchased, or should the prices be exorbitant, the purchases will be made elsewhere at fair rates. Collusion among dealers.

242. Articles and supplies purchased for the Service, before being accepted by the person authorized to receive them, must be carefully inspected, and will be rejected unless of good quality, corresponding to the specifications in the bid, and in every respect satisfactory. Inspection of supplies.

# REQUISITIONS

## MEDICAL SUPPLIES, BLANKS AND BOOKS, AND MISCELLANEOUS ARTICLES.

# REQUISITIONS FOR MEDICAL SUPPLIES, ETC.

243. Medical officers will, as far as practicable, anticipate the needs of the Service, at their respective stations, by making early requisition for such articles of hospital-furniture, bedding, clothing, medical supplies, or other property, as may be necessary.

Requisitions.

Form 1905.

244. Requisitions for medical supplies will be made semi-annually on the first days of October and April of each year, and shall be forwarded to the Supervising Surgeon-General.

Time of making.

Department Circular No. 31, Feb. 25, 1884.

245. The standard for medical supplies will be the medical-supply table of the Marine-Hospital Service.

Standard for medical supplies.

To permit the indulgence of individual preferences, and to provide for the exigencies of climate, season, epidemic diseases, &c., additional medicines may be required by the medical officer, who will then state the reasons for adding unusual articles and amounts.

246. When medical supplies require to be replenished at any time between the regular requisitions, special requisitions may be forwarded to the Supervising Surgeon-General, stating the articles and the quantities required up to the time when the next supply shall have been received.

Intermediate requisitions.

247. Requisitions for liquors and vials will be made on the 1st of October of each year for a supply for twelve months.

Liquors and vials.

Department Circular No. 31, Feb. 25, 1884.

248. Requisitions will be made semi-annually, on the 30th of June and the 31st of December of each year, by medical officers and acting assistant surgeons of the Marine-Hospital Service, for stationery, and on the 1st of April and the 1st of October of each year for blanks and books.

Stationery, blanks, and books.

Department Circular No. 113, Nov. 11, 1881.

249. In preparing requisitions for stationery, a full year's supply of ink and mucilage will be ordered on their July requisitions.

Ink.

250. Special requisitions will be made for such surgical instruments as may be necessary for the proper treatment of the patients of the Service, the instruments required to be enumerated and described.

Special requisitions; surgical instruments.

Form 1908.

Miscellaneous articles.

251. In special requisitions, each several item must be intelligibly described in the requisition, and the kind, quantity, or number, price, &c., of each article named. Items of different classes or character will not be included in one requisition. Furniture, bedding, clothing, repairs, &c., thus require separate requisitions, respectively.

To be accompanied by proposals.

252. Special requisitions for purchases or repairs on account of the Marine-Hospital Service will be accompanied by proposals from at least two responsible parties dealing in said articles, each stating the price at which he proposes to furnish the articles or make the repairs required; and no expenditure of this character will be incurred by medical officers or acting assistant surgeons of the Marine-Hospital Service without specific authority from the Department, except in cases of emergency. Requisitions should be made for each class of articles in order that they may be referred to the dealer or contractor for each separate class.

# EMERGENCY PURCHASES, REPAIRS, BILLS, ETC.

5 R R

253. When it is found impracticable to apply for and obtain the approval of the Department previous to making such purchases and repairs as may be absolutely necessary, bids in duplicate will nevertheless be obtained. The most advantageous bid will then be accepted; after which all the bids will be forwarded to the Department, accompanied by a statement of the reasons why special authority was not obtained previous to incurring the expenditure.

*Purchases in advance of approval, with bids.*

*R. S., s. 3710.*

254. For such absolutely necessary purchases and repairs as require immediate attention, and involve but small amounts, bids will not be required; but it must be satisfactorily shown that the expenditure was immediately necessary and could not have been foreseen by ordinary care, and the exigency must be certified on the face of the voucher.

*Emergency purchases.*

*R. S., s. 3709.*

255. Articles of subsistence not provided for by contract will be purchased by the hospital-steward, under the direction of the medical officer in charge, in open market, at the lowest market prices. Bills for articles purchased in open market must not be embraced in bills for articles purchased under contract.

*Purchase of subsistence in open market.*

256. All bills on account of the Marine-Hospital Service will be required to be rendered in duplicate, on the proper blanks. They must be itemized, and in cases where services or articles are furnished seamen the names of the latter must be given and the items specified, as far as practicable.

*Bills.*

*Forms 1937, 1938.*

*How rendered.*

257. Upon bills incurred under special authority from the Department, the particular authority for the expenditure will be referred to, and the dates of Department letters authorizing the payment of bills must be given.

*Authority to be cited.*

258. As far as practicable, every bill incurred on account of the Marine-Hospital Service, at any relief-station, will be obtained and promptly forwarded, as soon as contracted, to the Surgeon-General. Regular bills for articles purchased under contract will be forwarded at the close of each month.

*When to be rendered.*

259. Vouchers presented for payment must be in duplicate, properly certified, and receipted in black ink, and in-

*Preparation of vouchers for payment.*

dorsed and made in the name of the party, parties, firm, or corporation furnishing supplies or rendering service, and care should be taken that the signature to receipt conforms to the caption of the voucher.

Letters of transmittal.

260. Bills so forwarded will be accompanied by a letter giving the names of payees, the kind of articles purchased, and the amounts in each case, stating the necessity for the purchases made, &c., unless previously authorized.

Items to be classified.

261. Bills for items embraced in any special requisition approved by the Department must contain no other items.

Pay-rolls.

Form 1940.

262. Before the close of each month, surgeons in charge will make out pay-rolls, in duplicate, of the officers and employés, and forward them to the Supervising Surgeon-General. This provision does not apply to the stations on the Pacific coast or Key West, Fla., where the officers and employés will be paid by the customs officers on presentation of the pay-roll properly signed and certified.

Bills for maintenance.

Form 1923.

263. The monthly bills for the care and treatment of the patients of the Marine-Hospital Service, made out in duplicate upon blank, will be compared with the register of permits by the officer issuing hospital permits at each station, respectively, who will also muster the patients in hospital on the last day of each month, and certify the bills accordingly; and said bills will in no case be paid until they shall have been so compared, found correct, and certified.

Bills for medicines, &c.

264. The necessary medicines, surgical appliances, &c., furnished patients of the Marine-Hospital Service by apothecaries, upon the prescriptions of physicians authorized to prescribe for such patients, will be paid for at the lowest current and just prices charged the public at the time and place, bills to be rendered in due form by the apothecary, and certified by the physician and customs officer.

Name of seamen to be given on bills for prescriptions.

265. Bills for medicines dispensed for sick and disabled seamen, upon the prescriptions of medical officers or attending physicians, should state the names of seamen prescribed for, the dates, and the diagnoses, respectively.

## DISBURSEMENTS.

Customs officers to act as disbursing agents.

266. Bonded-customs officers are required, when so directed by the Secretary of the Treasury, to act as disbursing agents of the Marine-Hospital Service, and will pay, out of the funds remitted by the Treasury Department for that

purpose, bills on account of said Service previously authorized by the Department.

267. Upon the receipt of remittances, disbursing agents of the Marine-Hospital Service will promptly liquidate all authorized bills, and at the close of each month an account current of disbursements will be prepared and forwarded, showing the amounts disbursed during the month, said account to be accompanied by the proper abstract and vouchers. *Accounts current of disbursement. Form 1935.*

268. Accounts current of disbursements on account of the Marine-Hospital Service, with accompanying vouchers, may be forwarded without letters of transmittal, unless remarks or explanations concerning them are necessary. *How transmitted.*

## MISCELLANEOUS RECEIPTS.

269. Receipts accruing from the unclaimed moneys and effects of American seaman dying on shipboard without the United States, when deposited under the act of June 7, 1872, shall be credited to the appropriation for Marine-Hospital Service. *How deposited.*

270. Receipts accruing from the proceeds of sale of condemned and surplus property belonging to the Marine-Hospital Service shall be deposited as miscellaneous receipts. *Proceeds of miscellaneous sales.*

271. Receipts from the collection of bills for the care of foreign seamen, receipts from the sale or lease of marine-hospital property, and other miscellaneous receipts appropriated for the use of the Marine-Hospital Service, are not available for disbursements, and customs officers will accordingly render separate accounts each month for such receipts, accompanied by itemized abstracts. *Repayments for foreign seamen. Form 1926.*

272. Unclaimed money and valuable effects of deceased patients of the Marine-Hospital Service, at each relief-station, shall, at the close of each month, be delivered by the medical officer or acting assistant surgeon of the Service to the proper customs officer. *Unclaimed money of deceased seamen.*

273. The customs officer will sign triplicate receipts for such moneys deposited by medical officers, and will forward the original to the Department, the duplicate will be forwarded by the surgeon, and he will retain the triplicate as his personal voucher. In forwarding the duplicate, the medical officer will accompany it with a letter of trans- *Action upon.*

mittal, giving a descriptive-list of the deceased and the name of the vessel on which he last sailed.

Sundry accounts.   274. Separate accounts will be rendered covering receipts from unclaimed moneys and effects of seamen who die in hospital under the charge of the Marine-Hospital Service, which accounts must include no other items.

# RECORDS, REPORTS, AND CORRESPONDENCE.

# RECORDS, REPORTS, AND CORRESPONDENCE.

## RECORDS.

275. The following-named official records shall be kept at all relief-stations of the first class, viz : A register of out-patients, (Form 1944 ;) a register of hospital patients, (Form 1945 ;) a record of moneys and valuables of hospital patients, (Form 1950 ;) a journal, (Form 1955 ;) a record of medical inspections of seamen, (Form 1956 ;) a record of letters and papers received, (Form 1957 ;) and a record of letters and papers sent, (Form 1958.) And where there are marine hospitals the following in addition, viz: An inventory of patients' effects, (Form 1949 ;) a record of subsistence and other supplies, (Form 1951 ;) an inventory of furniture, (Form 1952 ;) an inventory of medical supplies, (Form 1953 ;) and a record of liquors consumed, (Form 1952.)

*Stations of first class.*

276. Medical officers and acting assistant surgeons of the Marine-Hospital Service, and other physicians having hospital patients of that Service under their professional care, shall keep a register of hospital patients, (Form 1946 ;) a prescription and diet book, (Form 1948 ;) and a case-book, (Form 1947.)

*Professional records.*

277. Collectors of customs will keep the register of permits, (Form 1945 ;) the register of out-patients, (Form 1944 ;) and the record of moneys and valuables of hospital patients (Form 1650) at all relief-stations of the second class, except that in cases where the acting assistant surgeons are on duty at said stations, the latter shall keep the register of out-patients, and will keep the register of permits when so authorized and directed by the Secretary of the Treasury.

*Collectors of customs.*

278. The Register of Out-Patients shall contain the number, (commencing with No. 1 on the 1st July of each year,) name, age, and nativity of each patient; the name of the vessel on which he last served, and the period of his last service; the patient's statement as to any previous relief from the Marine-Hospital Service, and when, where, and for what disease such relief was obtained; present disease or injury; dates on which out-door relief is extended, and

*Register of Out-Patients.*

*Form 1944.*

the kind of relief furnished.   Only one entry of each patient will be made during any current month when relieved
for the same disease or injury; but, when relief is furnished
several times during the month for the same disease or injury, the date and the kind of relief will be entered each
time in the same place.   A seaman who has received office-
relief for some one disease or injury and applies again in
the same month for relief on account of some other disease
or injury, will be re-entered as a new case, if again relieved
as an out-patient.   An out-patient relieved two or more
successive months for the same disease will be re-entered
on the register each month as remaining from the previous
month.

Register of
Hospital Pa-
tients.

Form 1495.

279.  The Register of Hospital Patients, to be kept in the
marine-hospital office, shall contain the number and date
of the permit, (or of the bed-ticket in the case of United
States marine hospitals;) the name, age, and nativity of
the patient; the name of the vessel on which he last served;
the total period of his last service; the number of years he
has been an American seaman; the disease or injury for
the treatment of which the permit is issued; the date of
termination of treatment, and any necessary remarks.

Register of
Hospital Pa-
tients.

Form 1946.

280.  The Register of Hospital Patients shall contain the
number of the permit; the name, age, and nativity of the
patient; the date of admission; the disease or injury; subsequent complications, if any; date of letter authorizing
extension of original permit; date of termination of treatment; condition of patient on termination of treatment;
total duration of treatment in hospital under the permit,
and any necessary remarks.

Case-Book.

Form 1947.

281.  The Case-Book shall contain a full record of each
important and instructive case, describing its cause, progress, treatment, and termination.

Prescription
and Diet Book.

Form 1948.

282.  In the Prescription and Diet Book shall be entered
the prescriptions, and the kind of diet ordered for each
hospital patient.

283.  A Register of Out-Patients, Register of Hospital
Permits, Register of Hospital Patients, Case-Book, or Prescription and Diet Book, will not be required to be kept at
relief-stations of the third class.

Journal of
stations.

Form 1955.

284.  In the Journal shall be recorded the dates of changes
of officers or employés; repairs or alterations of buildings;
construction of new buildings; changes in the arrangements
for the care of patients at ports where there are no United

States marine hospitals; any marked changes in the Service for each month; the breaking out of an epidemic; and any other events of interest and importance.

285. A record will be kept of all medical inspections of seamen, and a transcript of said record will be forwarded quarterly to the Supervising Surgeon-General.

*Record of medical inspections of seamen.*

*Form 1953.*

### PERIODICAL REPORTS TO BE MADE.

286. Medical officers and acting assistant surgeons will make the following-named reports, viz: Monthly reports of the current transactions of the Service, and monthly reports of relief furnished seamen not contributors to the marine-hospital fund. The latter report will also be made by acting assistant surgeons on duty at stations of the second class.

*Monthly reports.*

*Forms 1919, 1925.*

287. Medical officers and acting assistant surgeons of the Marine-Hospital Service, and other physicians having charge of the professional treatment of patients of that Service, will make monthly reports of all cases of disease and injury treated by them in hospital, and of all cases of disease and injury treated in the out-patient department. They will also make, on the 30th of June of each year, annual reports of the surgical operations performed by them upon patients of the Marine-Hospital Service.

*Forms 1920, 1921, 1922.*

288. Letter-press copies will be taken of all official letters written by medical officers, and retained copies of all official reports shall be kept on file at the marine-hospital or surgeon's office.

*Copies of reports and letters.*

289. Whenever at any time there are no transactions to be stated in any report, account, or other return required by these regulations to be periodically rendered, the words "No transactions" will be written across the face of the blank form in each case, which will then be dated, signed, briefed, and forwarded.

*"No transactions."*

290. When communications are referred from an office, the reference should be made on the first fold, if there be sufficient space; otherwise, on the following fold. Indorsements should not be made on separate pieces of paper and attached in any way, unless all the folds of a paper are full and in that case the added paper should be securely attached in such manner as not to cover a previous indorsement or place where one might have been made.

*Indorsements and references.*

Letters of transmittal.

291. Regular reports rendered under these regulations, and other papers which are in themselves communications, require no letters of transmittal. Special requisitions, estimates, proposals, and bills, however, will always be accompanied by letters, giving briefly such information as may be necessary for proper action thereon.

Official files.

292. All official letters and documents received are required to be kept on file by medical officers and acting assistant surgeons of the Marine-Hospital Service, unless otherwise directed, and will be carefully preserved in proper order.

Ink.

293. All communications to the Department must be written in black ink.

Official forms to be used.

294. All returns, vouchers, reports, and other official papers required under these regulations must be made out in conformity therewith, upon the blank forms furnished by the Treasury Department for that purpose.

### CORRESPONDENCE.

Acknowledgment of orders.

295. The receipt by a medical officer or acting assistant surgeon of the Marine-Hospital Service of any official order from the Department will in each case be acknowledged by return mail, but when orders are given by telegraph the answer should also be sent by telegraph.

Official signatures.

296. Official papers, reports, and letters of medical officers and acting assistant surgeons will be in due official form, and signed over the official designation or title of the writer, and each letter will, as far as practicable, cover but one subject. Personal matters will not be included in official communications.

Department circulars.

297. In referring to a Department circular relating to the Marine-Hospital Service, medical officers and acting assistant surgeons of that Service will give its date and number in the annual series of the Marine-Hospital Service.

Replies to Department letters.

298. In replying to an official letter from the Department, the date of said letter, its subject-matter, and the initials on the upper left-hand corner will be referred to.

Manner of addressing official letters to Department.

299. Every letter, report, or other paper addressed to the Department, or intended to be placed on file, should show on the inside the name or title of the officer addressed, the date when written, and the signature of the writer, with his official title, and be paged.

Communications on letter paper should be folded in three (3) folds, and those on foolscap paper in four (4) folds, and briefed by the writer, or sender, on the first or upper fold, as follows:

I. The place where the communication was written, and the date.

II. The name and official designation, if any, of the writer.

III. A brief of the subject-matter, embracing everything of importance, particularly the names of persons mentioned.

At the top of the fold a space of an inch should be left blank, and the number or enclosures should be noted at the bottom. In stating the number of enclosures, the communication itself will not be counted as an enclosure.

300. Abbreviations of words will be avoided in all official letters and papers. In the use of the telegraph all superfluous words will be omitted from the body of the telegram, and the addresses and signatures will be condensed as much as possible.

Abbreviations.

# TONNAGE-DUES.

# TONNAGE-DUES.

301. Customs officers will collect from vessels arriving in the United States from any foreign port of North America north of the southern terminus of the Isthmus of Darien, or any port in Newfoundland, the West Indian, Bahama, Bermuda, or Sandwich Islands, a duty of three cents per ton on every entry; but the total tax in any one year on entries from the ports specified is not to exceed fifteen cents. The tax to be collected on vessels making entry on arrival from other foreign ports is six cents per ton on every entry; but the total tax collected at six cents per ton is not to exceed thirty cents per ton in any one year. Rates for assessment.

U. S. Stat., c. 121, 1884, act June 26.

302. Any vessel making such voyages as to become liable in any one year under both rates—that is, at three cents per ton and six cents per ton—shall not be held liable to an aggregate tax of more than thirty cents per ton for any one year, reckoned from the date of the entry and payment of her first tax at either rate; but the three-cent tax per ton shall not be collected on more than five entries in any one year. Number of times tax may be assessed.

303. For half a ton or more than half a ton of the measurement of a vessel, collection will be made at the full rates of three or six cents per ton; for less than half a ton no collection will be made. Small craft exempt.

304. As provided by the act of June 26, 1884, "that the President of the United States shall suspend the collection of so much of the duty herein imposed on vessels entered from any port in the Dominion of Canada, Newfoundland, the Bahama Islands, the Bermuda Islands, the West India Islands, Mexico, and Central America down to and including Aspinwall and Panama, as may be in excess of the tonnage and light-house dues, or other equivalent tax or taxes, imposed on American vessels by the government of the foreign country in which such port is situated, and shall upon the passage of this act, and from time to time thereafter as often as it may become necessary by reason of changes in the laws of the foreign countries above men- Dues suspended reciprocally.

6 R R

tioned, indicate by proclamation the ports to which such suspension shall apply, and the rate or rates of tonnage duty, if any, to be collected under such suspension ;" but customs officers will take no action by way of suspension of collection of tax till they have been informed that such suspension has been authorized by a proclamation of the President.

Reports to be made.

305. Customs officers will forward at the close of each month, for the information of the Marine-Hospital Bureau,

Department Circular No. 120, July 22, 1884.

a summary statement of the aggregate collections of ton-nage-tax at their ports during the month.

# MISCELLANEOUS.

306. No medical officer shall receive, have charge of, or pay any money on account of the Marine-Hospital Service, except the money belonging to patients of the Service, as prescribed in these regulations. Officers not to pay money.

307. No medical officer or acting assistant surgeon of the Marine-Hospital Service shall, either directly or indirectly, receive any pay or emolument, or have any pecuniary or material interest in, or benefit from, any hospital in which patients of the Marine-Hospital Service are cared for. Officers not to have interest in contract hospitals.

308. Medical officers and acting assistant surgeons of the Marine-Hospital Service will, for all official medical and pharmacal purposes, make use of the metric system of weights and measures. In expressing quantities by weight, the terms "gram" and "centigram" only will be used, and in expressing quantities by measure the term "cubic centimetre." Metric system.

309. In recording thermometric observations, medical officers and acting assistant surgeons of the Marine-Hospital Service will make use of and refer to the centigrade scale only. Centigrade scale.

310. In preparing the medical and surgical reports, and all medical certificates, the official nomenclature of diseases adopted for the Marine-Hospital Service will be observed, and the English names of diseases and injuries used, in the order given in said nomenclature. Nomenclature of diseases.

311. Medicines will be allowed medical officers for themselves and their families when sick, but they will not be allowed other hospital supplies. Medical officers on duty in United States marine hospitals may, however, be furnished subsistence for themselves and their families in extraordinary cases, when specially authorized by the Department, but in such event, the officer will reimburse the Service the proper cost thereof. Officers allowed medical supplies.

312. Quarters or subsistence will not be furnished in United States marine hospitals to persons who are not employed therein by authority of the Treasury Department, Quarters for unauthorized persons.

except in extraordinary cases, upon specific authority from the Secretary of the Treasury in each case.

**Official seal.** 313. All official certificates issued by medical officers of the Marine-Hospital Service, under these regulations, will be stamped with the official seal of the Service.

**Officers not to publish statistics, &c., without authority.** 314. Medical officers and acting assistant surgeons will not publish or furnish for publication any official reports or current statistics of the operations of the Service without authority from the Supervising Surgeon-General; but this is not to be construed as applicable to purely professional subjects based upon original investigations of disease as seen among seamen or others.

**Officers not to keep animals for private use.** 315. Medical officers and acting assistant surgeons will not be permitted to keep within the hospital grounds any animal for their own use without permission of the Supervising Surgeon-General, nor will they allow any other than authorized animals to be so kept.

**No advertisement without authority.** 316. Advertisements will be inserted in such newspapers only as the Secretary of the Treasury may direct, and no bill for any such advertising will be paid, unless there be presented with such bill, the original, or a copy of such written authority.

**R. S., 1878, p. 749, s. 3828.**
**15 July, 1870. c. 292, s. 2, v. 16, p. 308.**

**Death of officers.** 317. In the case of the death of an officer or other person employed in the Marine-Hospital Service, or of any person having claims against the United States on account of the Marine-Hospital Service, payments, when duly authorized, are only to be made to the legal representative of such person, according to the forms of law. No departure from this rule will be sanctioned, unless authorized by instructions from the Secretary of the Treasury, to whom a report of the case, together with the reasons for dispensing with legal forms, must first be transmitted by the disbursing agent.

**Telegraphing.** 318. Whenever it shall be necessary for medical officers or acting assistant surgeons of the Marine-Hospital Service to make use of the telegraph in sending messages to the Department, due care will be taken to make the same as brief as is consistent with clearness.

**Freight shipments prepaid.** 319. On shipments made by the Supervising Surgeon-General the freight or express charges will be prepaid in all cases where practicable; but the drayage or other charges attending the transfer of goods from the depot or wharf at the point of destination, and the freight or express charges, if not prepaid, must be paid by the officer receiving the shipment, and will be refunded upon receipt of bills, accompanied by sub-vouchers covering the full amount charged.

320. When stationery or books and blanks are forwarded by express, the charges thereon are invariably prepaid by the Department; but on all shipments by freight the charges are to be paid by the officer receiving the goods, who will forward the freight-bills to the Department, when authority will be given the proper disbursing agent to re-imburse him. *Stationery shipments by express and freight.*

321. At stations where no medical officer or acting assistant surgeon of the Marine-Hospital Service is on duty, the proper customs officer will have custody of all property belonging to the Marine-Hospital Service, and will account for the same to the Treasury Department. *Customs officers to have custody of property.*

# GOVERNMENT OF NATIONAL QUARANTINES.

# GOVERNMENT OF NATIONAL QUARANTINES.

322. At ports where quarantine may be established by the Secretary of the Treasury, every vessel, before being permitted to enter, shall present to the collector of customs satisfactory evidence either that said vessel had not, at any time during a period of thirty days immediately preceding its arrival, touched at or communicated with any foreign port where cholera, yellow fever, or small-pox was known to exist in an epidemic form ; that there had not been at any time during that period any case of contagious disease on board ; and that said vessel does not convey any person or persons, merchandise, or animals affected with any infectious or contagious disease, or that the said vessel has been thoroughly cleaned and disinfected by the quarantine officer, and is free from infection at the time of entry. The certificate to that effect. of the medical officer of the Marine-Hospital Service, or other agent of the Treasury Department designated by the Secretary of the Treasury to act as quarantine officer for the United States at the port, shall be accepted by the collector of customs as satisfactory evidence, and the medical officer or agent referred to shall, before granting such certificate, satisfy himself that the matters and things therein stated are true.

Vessels required to present evidence of being free from contagious diseases before entry.

Section 5, act April 29, 1878. R. S., s. 4792.

323. Vessels coming from a foreign port or country where cholera, yellow fever, or small-pox is known to have existed in an epidemic form within thirty days preceding their arrival, and vessels or vehicles conveying any person or persons, merchandise, or animals affected with any contagious disease, or having had on board at any time during the thirty days preceding their arrival any case of contagious disease, shall not enter any port of the United States until such disinfection or other precautionary measures shall have been performed as prescribed by these regulations, and the certificate of the medical officer of the Marine-Hospital Service, or other designated agent of the Treasury Department, shall, in such cases, as in the cases referred to in the preceding paragraph, be accepted by the collector

Vessels from infected ports not allowed to enter until certificate of free pratique is furnished.

of customs as satisfactory evidence of compliance with said regulations.

**Infected vessels required to anchor at quarantine station.** 324. For purposes of necessary disinfection of a vessel and its cargo, and of the clothing and baggage of persons on board, the said vessel shall be required to repair to and cast anchor at such place as may be designated by the Secretary of the Treasury, at each port respectively, to be known as the United States Quarantine Station.

**Methods of disinfection.** 325. The disinfection, and other precautionary measures referred to in paragraph 323, shall be carried out under the direction and supervision of the United States quarantine officer at each port respectively, and shall consist of, first, the isolation and treatment of the sick; second, the disinfection of all clothing and baggage liable to be infected; third, the removal of the cargo from the vessel to open lighters, and its thorough disinfection by chemical agents, by exposure to free currents of air, or by burning, as the case may require; and, fourth, the cleansing and fumigation of the vessel, or such other methods of disinfection as may from time to time be adopted by the Department.

# APPENDIX.

# INSTRUCTIONS

RELATIVE TO THE

## PHYSICAL EXAMINATION OF SEAMEN.

# INSTRUCTIONS RELATIVE TO PHYSICAL EXAMI-
## NATION OF SEAMEN.

I. Medical officers of the Marine-Hospital Service, detailed to conduct the physical examination required by paragraph 80 of the Regulations, will be guided by the following general directions:

II. Any one of the following defects will be sufficient cause for rejection, viz: Decided cachexia; strumous diathesis, or apparent predisposition to any constitutional disease; permanent defects of either of the extremities or articulations, causing inefficiency; unnatural excurvature or incurvature of the spine; impaired vision; color-blindness; myopia; chronic disease of the visual organs; epilepsy; insanity; apparent tendency to convulsions; chronic disease of the ears; deafness; chronic nasal catarrh; polypi; chronic tonsilar enlargement; chronic ulcers, or cicatrices of old ulcers likely to break out afresh; chronic cardiac affections; insufficient chest expansion; hernia; sarcocele; hydrocele; varicocele, unless slight; stricture of the urethra or rectum; fistula; hæmorrhoids; varicose veins of lower limbs, unless slight; stature less than five feet.

III. Besides the above, the existence of any disease, physical deformity, or abnormal condition of such character as to incapacitate the candidate for the performance of his duties, will be cause for rejection.

IV. In making the examinations, medical officers will be guided by the following special directions, which are slightly modified from those in force in the United States Army:

1. In physical examinations of officers. as preliminary to promotion, and of enlisted men, as preliminary to re-enlistment, the clothing may or may not be removed, at the discretion of the examining surgeon.

2. In case the disease or disability for which an applicant was rejected is temporary in its character, the rejection at such examination shall not debar him from subsequent examination, in case he claims that the disease for which he was rejected has disappeared.

3. The applicant will be required to divest himself of all his clothing, in the presence of the examining surgeon, so that any defect, as a stiff

7 R R

joint, &c., which the applicant would wish to conceal, may be detected, especially as he will be thrown off his guard, not supposing the examination had commenced.   Having divested himself of his clothing, the candidate should be asked his name, age, nativity, and occupation, and questioned in regard to his general health and that of his family, whether any hereditary taints exist, and if he has ever suffered from any disease or accident, thus endeavoring to obtain all the information possible concerning him, his conversation at the same time enabling the surgeon to judge of his mental qualifications.   He will then be placed under the sliding bar of a stationary measuring-rod, directed to stand erect while his height will be accurately measured, together with the body length.   The height measure will be taken while the toes are raised, the candidate resting the foot squarely upon the heel and ball of the foot.   A tape-measure will be passed around the chest over the inferior angles of the scapula, and directly over the nipples, and an accurate measurement taken both at inspiration and expiration.   The tape will be passed around the chest while both arms are extended at a right angle from the sides, and the arms will then be dropped to the side while the measurements are taken.   After this, the color of the eyes and hair and the complexion should be noted, and a general inspection of the whole body made, notice being taken of the muscular development and general appearance; and at the same time tumors, ulcers, varicose veins, chronic swellings of the extremities, or any visible defect that would disqualify him for service should be carefully sought for. The head will then be examined for any depressions or irregularities that may exist, and the eyes, eyelids, nose, ears, teeth, palate, and fauces attentively noticed.   The chest will then be inspected, and the respiration, action of the heart, and condition of the lungs, ascertained by auscultation and percussion.   He will next be directed to stand erect, place his heels together, and raise his hands vertically above his head, the backs together, in which position he will be required to cough and make other expulsive movements, while the abdomen, the inguinal rings, and the scrotum are being examined for hernia.   The penis will then be examined for epispadia, hypospadia, and venereal disease; the groin for glandular enlargements; and testicles for atrophy, induration, and other diseases.   He will then be required to bend forward, the fingers touching the floor, the legs straight, and the feet widely separated, in which position the fissure between the nates will be inspected for hæmorrhoids, fistula, prolapsus, or other disease of the anus, and firm pressure will be made along the whole length of the spine, at short intervals, to discover if any tenderness indicative of disease exists. Next he will be required to extend his arms laterally, at right angles to the body, and then bring them together on as nearly the same level as possible both in front and behind; to pronate and supinate them rapidly; to strike out from the shoulder; to flex the arm upon the shoulder, and the forearm upon the arm; and to open and close the fingers rapidly. He will then be required to walk rapidly and to run around the room several times; to hop, first on one foot and then on the other; with his heels together, to raise himself upon his toes; to flex and extend the thigh, leg, and foot; to kick, first with one foot and then with the other, and to make several leaps in the air. While thus excited he will again be examined for lung and heart diseases, also for hernia.

In making the examination of the inguinal rings the surgeon will use the index finger of the hand corresponding to the side examined, thus: for the right ring, the right index finger, and *vice versa*. The eyesight will be tested by the test types furnished by the Department, and the Holmgren worsted test will be employed in testing for color-blindness. The test must be made for each eye separately. The hearing will also be tested by modulating the tones of the voice in conversation with the applicant, and by covering one ear while endeavoring to discover defects of the other. The result of the examination will then be recorded, and, in case of rejection, the disease or infirmity on account of which he was found unfit for service will be written in full in the book prepared for that purpose.

# DIRECTIONS

## FOR

## RESTORING THE APPARENTLY DROWNED.

# DIRECTIONS FOR RESTORING THE APPARENTLY DROWNED.*

RULE I. *Arouse the patient.*—Unless in danger of freezing, do not move the patient, but instantly expose the face to a current of fresh air, wipe dry the mouth and nostrils, rip the clothing, so as to expose the chest and waist, and give two or three quick smarting slaps on the stomach and chest with the open hand. If, however, there is reason to believe that considerable time has elapsed since the patient became insensible, do not lose further time by practising Rule I, but proceed immediately to Rule II. After loosening clothing, &c., if the patient does not revive, then proceed thus:

RULE. II. *To expel water, &c., from the stomach and chest.*—(See

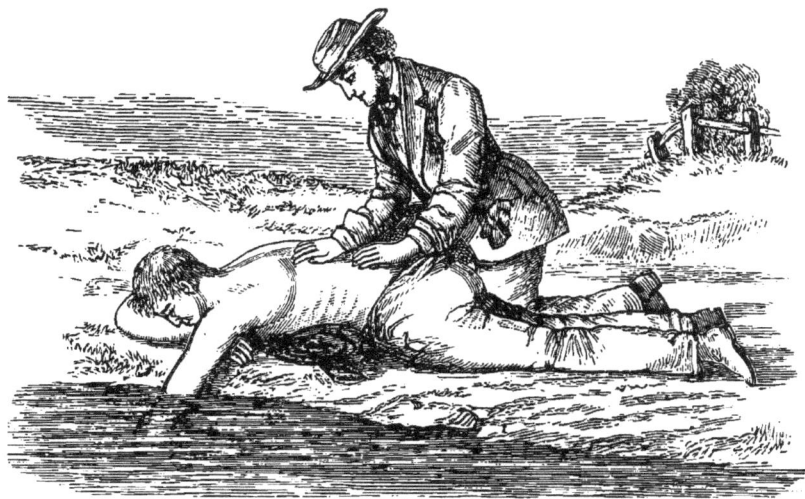

FIG. I. *Showing the first step taken, by which the chest is emptied of air, and the ejection of any fluids swallowed is assisted.*

Fig. 1.)—If the jaws are clenched, separate them, and keep the mouth open by placing between the teeth a cork or small bit of wood; turn the patient on the face, a large bundle of tightly-rolled clothing being placed beneath the stomach, and press heavily over it for half a minute, or so long as fluids flow freely from the mouth.

---

*From the Regulations of the United States Life-Saving Service.

RULE III. *To produce breathing.*—(See. Fig II.)—Clear the mouth and throat of mucus, by introducing into the throat the corner of a handkerchief wrapped closely around the forefinger; turn the patient

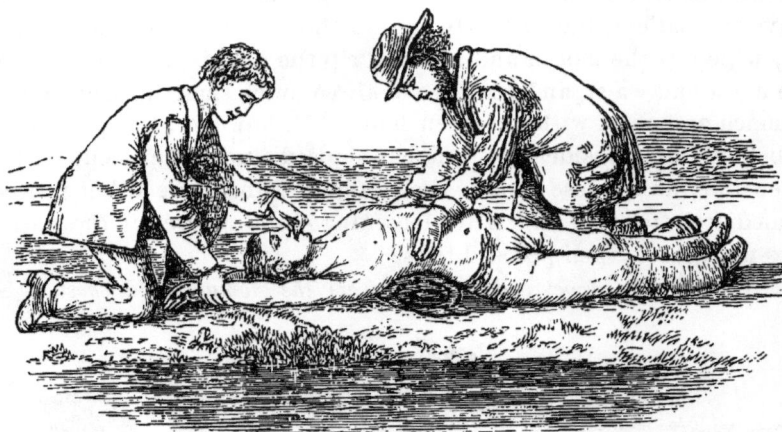

FIG. II. *Showing the position and action of the operator, in alternately producing artificial expiration and inspiration of air.*

on the back, the roll of clothing being so placed beneath it as to raise the pit of the stomach above the level of any other part of the body. If there be another person present, let him, with a piece of dry cloth, hold the tip of the tongue out of one corner of the mouth, (this prevents the tongue from falling back and choking the entrance to the windpipe,) and with the other hand grasp both wrists and keep the arms forcibly stretched back above the head, thereby increasing the prominence of the ribs, which tends to enlarge the chest. The two last-named positions are not, however, absolutely essential to success. Kneel beside or astride the patient's hips, and with the balls of the thumbs resting on either side of the pit of the stomach, let the fingers fall into the grooves between the short ribs, so as to afford the best grasp of the waist. Now, using your knees as a pivot, throw all your weight forward on your hands, and at the same time squeeze the waist between them as if you wished to force everything in the chest upward out of the mouth; deepen the pressure while you can count slowly one, two, three; then suddenly let go with a final push, which springs you back to your first kneeling position. Remain erect on your knees while you can count one, two, three; then repeat the same motions as before at a rate gradually increased from four or five to fifteen times in a minute, and continue thus this bellows movement with the same regularity that is observable in the natural motions of breathing which you are imitating. If natural breathing be not restored, after a trial of the bellows movement for the space of three or four minutes, then turn the patient a second time on the stomach, as directed in Rule II, rolling the body in the opposite direction from that in which it was first turned, for the purpose of freeing the air-passages from any remaining water. Continue the artificial respiration from one to four hours, or until the patient breathes, according to Rule III; and for a while, after the appearance of returning life, carefully aid the first short gasps until deepened into full breaths. Continue the drying and rubbing, which should have been unceasingly practised from the beginning by the assistants, taking care not to interfere with the means employed to produce breathing. Thus the limbs of the patient should be rubbed, always in an upward direction towards the body, with firm grasping pressure and energy, using the bare hands, dry flannels, or handkerchiefs, and continuing the friction under the blankets or over the dry clothing. The warmth of the body can also be promoted by the application of hot flannels to the stomach and arm-pits, bottles or bladders of hot water, heated bricks, &c., to the limbs and soles of the feet.

RULE IV. AFTER-TREATMENT.—*Externally:* As soon as breathing is established, let the patient be stripped of all wet clothing, wrapped in blankets only, put to bed comfortably warm, but with a free circularion of fresh air, and left to perfect rest. *Internally:* Give whiskey or brandy and hot water in doses of a teaspoonful to a tablespoonful, according to the weight of the patient, or other stimulant at hand, every ten or fifteen minutes for the first hour, and as often thereafter as may seem expedient. *Later manifestations:* After reaction is fully established, there is great danger of congestion of the lungs, and if perfect rest is not maintained for at least forty-eight hours, it sometimes occurs that the patient is seized with great difficulty of breathing, and death is liable to follow unless immediate relief is afforded. In such cases apply a large mustard-plaster over the breast. If the patient gasps for breath before the mustard takes effect, assist the breathing by carefully repeating the artificial respiration.

NOTE.—It has been shown that the clenching of the jaws and the semi-contraction of the fingers, which have hitherto been considered signs of death, are, in fact, evidences of remaining vitality. After numerous experiments with apparently drowned persons, and also with animals, Labordette states that these are only signs accompanying the first stage of suffocation by drowning, the jaws and hands becoming relaxed when death ensues.* This being so, the mere clenching

---

* The muscular rigidity of death (*rigor mortis*) occurs later, after the temporary relaxation here referred to.

of the jaws and semi-contraction of the hands must not be considered as reasons for the discontinuance of efforts to save life, but should serve as a stimulant to vigorous and prolonged efforts to quicken vitality.   Persons engaged in the tasks of resuscitation are, therefore, earnestly desired to take hope and encouragement for the life of the sufferer, from the signs above referred to, and to continue their endeavors accordingly.   In a number of cases Dr. Labordette restored to life persons whose jaws were so firmly clenched that, to aid respiration, their teeth had to be forced apart with iron instruments.

# DIET-TABLE.

The following diet-table will be observed in all United States marine hospitals, with such modifications only as climate and season may render necessary:

## I.—ORDINARY DIET-TABLE—UNITED STATES MARINE HOSPITALS.

| | MONDAY. | TUESDAY. | WEDNESDAY. | THURSDAY. | FRIDAY. | SATURDAY. | SUNDAY. |
|---|---|---|---|---|---|---|---|
| **Breakfast.** | Coffee....pt. 1<br>Bread....oz. 6<br>Butter....oz. ½<br>Meat-hash, with vegetables....oz. 6<br>*Stewed fruit....oz. 3 | Coffee....pt. 1<br>Bread....oz. 6<br>Butter....oz. ½<br>Corned-beef hash, with potatoes....oz. 6<br>....oz. 3 | Coffee....pt. 1<br>Bread....oz. 4<br>Butter....oz. ½<br>Fish-hash, with vegetables....oz. 6 | Coffee....pt. 1<br>Bread....oz. 6<br>Butter....oz. ¾<br>Meat-stew....oz. 6 | Coffee....pt. 1<br>Bread....oz. 6<br>Butter....oz. ½<br>Fish-hash, with vegetables....oz. 6 | Coffee....pt. 1<br>Bread....oz. 6<br>Butter....oz. ½<br>Mutton-chops....oz. 6<br>Fried potatoes....oz. 3 | Chocolate....pt. 1<br>Bread....oz. 6<br>Butter....oz. ½<br>Meat-stew....oz. 4<br>Fruit-sauce....oz. 3 |
| **Dinner.** | Vegetable-soup....pt. 1<br>Beef, boiled....oz. 6<br>Potatoes....oz. 8<br>Pudding, with sauce....oz. 4<br>Bread....oz. 4 | Beef-soup....pt. 1<br>Beef, boiled....oz. 6<br>Fish, fresh....oz. 8<br>Vegetables....oz.<br>Bread....oz. 4<br>Fruit....oz. 4 | Mutton-broth....pt. 1<br>Mutton, boiled....oz. 6<br>Potatoes....oz. 8<br>Rice-pudding, with sauce....oz. 8<br>Bread....oz. 4 | Soup, bouillon....pt. 1<br>Beef, roast....oz. 6<br>Potatoes....oz. 8<br>Bread....oz. 4<br>Fruit....oz. 4 | Vegetable-soup....pt. 1<br>Meat-stew....oz. 6<br>Fish....oz. 8<br>Bread....oz. 8<br>Vegetables....oz. 4<br>Fruit....oz. 4 | Barley-soup....pt. 1<br>Mutton, boiled....oz. 8<br>Bread....oz. 6<br>Vegetables....oz. 10 | Soup....pt. 1<br>Beef, roast....oz. 6<br>Potatoes....oz. 8<br>Other vegetables....oz. 4<br>Rice, or tapioca-pudding....oz. 4 |
| **Supper.** | Tea....pt. 1<br>Bread....oz. 6<br>Butter....oz. ½<br>Fruit-sauce....oz. 3 | Tea....pt. 1<br>Bread....oz. 6<br>Butter....oz. ½<br>*Fruit, stewed....oz. 3 | Tea....pt. 1<br>Bread....oz. 6<br>Butter....oz. ½<br>Cooked fruit....oz. 4 | Tea....pt. 1<br>Bread....oz. 6<br>Butter....oz. ½<br>Fruit-pudding....oz. 4 | Tea....pt. 1<br>Bread....oz. 4<br>Butter....oz. ¾<br>Cold meat....oz. 4 | Tea....pt. 1<br>Bread....oz. 4<br>Butter....oz. ¾<br>Rice, with sauce or sirup....oz. 4 | Tea....pt. 1<br>Bread....oz. 6<br>Butter....oz. ¾<br>Mush and milk....oz. 12 |

*Fresh fruit may be substituted in season.

NOTE.—The tea and coffee prepared with milk and sugar.

The quantities of the articles of diet indicate them as they are prepared ready to serve.

The above table gives the four classes of solid constituents in substantially the following proportions: NITROGENOUS or PLASTIC MATERIAL, about 140 grams; FAT, about 62 grams; CARBO-HYDRATES, (starch, sugar, &c.,) about 450 grams; and SALINES, about 2,250 grams of water. Although these quantities are somewhat in excess of the estimates for "healthy adults at rest," they are none too great for convalescents in whom tissue-metamorphosis is being carried on, not only in the interest of repair of present waste from use, but in the interest of repair of past waste from disease, a point which should not be over-looked in the construction of hospital dietaries. In making any change from the above, the substituted articles should be in such quantities and of such kinds as to furnish constituents equivalent to those of the articles replaced.

## II.—EXTRA DIET.

|  |  |  |
|---|---|---|
| For breakfast......... | { Mutton-chop, or } ...... Beef-steak........... } | ounces... 6 |
|  | { Eggs........... | number... 2 |
| Dinner .................. | { Chicken, or } ...... Game........... } | ounces 6 |
|  | { Ale or wine .................. | — |
| Supper .................. | Dry or dip toast.................. | ounces... 4 |

## III.—MILK DIET.

|  |  |  |
|---|---|---|
| Breakfast............. | { Hominy, or } ...... Corn-meal mush... } | ounces... 14 |
|  | { Milk.................. | ounces... 16 |
| Dinner .................. | { Rice or tapioca, (cooked).................. | ounces... 12 |
|  | { Milk.................. | ounces... 16 |
|  | { Sirup.................. | ounces... 1 |
|  | { Bread .................. | ounces... 4 |
|  | { Butter.................. | ounce... ½ |
| Supper .................. | { Cracked wheat, or } when cooked,...... Oaten grits............. } | ounces... 14 |
|  | { Toasted bread .................. | ounces... 12 |
|  | { Milk.................. | ounces... 16 |

# BLANKS AND BOOKS.

## BLANKS.

No.
1901. Oath of office. (10 by 8.)
1902. Official bond. (13 by 8.)
1903. Property return, (United States marine hospitals.) (17 leaves, 14 by 8.)
1904. Property return, (for officers not in charge U. S. marine hospitals.) (8 leaves, 14 by 8.)
1905. Requisition for medical supplies. (14 by 8.)
1906. Requisition for blanks and blank books. (10 by 8.)
1907. Requisition for stationery. (14 by 8.)
1908. Special requisition, (miscellaneous.) (14 by 8.)
1909. Report of inspection of property. (16 by 24.)
1910. Annual estimate of subsistence and other supplies. (14 by 8.)
1911. Schedule of and proposal to furnish subsistence and other supplies. (14 by 8.)
1912. Contract to furnish subsistence and other supplies. (13 by 8.)
1913. Monthly report of subsistence and other supplies. (14 by 8.)
1914. Master's certificate of seaman's service. (7 by 8.)
1915. Relief certificate. (10 by 8.)
1916. Hospital permit. (10 by 8.)
1916½. Certificate of discharge. (5 by 6.)
1917. Bed-ticket. (5 by 3.)
1917½. Daily diet list. (14 by 8.)
1918. Application for extension of permit. (10 by 8.)
1919. Medical officers' monthly report of relief. (14 by 8.)
1920. Medical and surgical report of out-patients. (14 by 8.)
1921. Medical and surgical report of hospital patients. (14 by 8.)
1921½. Clinical record. (8 by 22.)
1922. Annual report of surgical operations. (14 by 17.)
1923. Bill for the care of seamen. (16 by 10.)
1924. Report of admission of seamen not paying marine-hospital dues. (10 by 8.)
1925. Report of relief furnished seamen not contributing to the marine-hospital fund. (10 by 8.)
1926. Bill for care of foreign seamen. (7 by 8.)
1927. Proposal to furnish care and treatment to sick seamen. (10 by 8.)
1928. Certificate of medical inspection of seamen. (10 by 8.)
1929. Transcript of record of medical inspections of seamen, (quarterly.) (14 by 17.)
1937. Bill. (14 by 8.)
1938. Bill. (10 by 8.)
1939. Pay-roll. (16 by 10.)
1940. Pay-roll. (8 by 10.)
1941. Voucher for travelling expenses. (10 by 8.)
1942. Daily report of seamen admitted and discharged. (8 by 14.)
1971. Weekly abstract of bills of health.
1974. Consular sanitary report, (to Secretary of State.) (5 by 8.)

## BOOKS.

1944. Register of out-patients. (3 quires, 15 by 10.)
1945. Register of permits. (200 leaves, 16 by 10.)
1946. Register of hospital patients. (4 quires, 11 by 8.)
1947. Case-book. (3 quires, 10 by 8.)
1948a. Prescription and diet book. (5 quires, 16 by 10.)
1948b. Prescription and diet book. (2 quires, 16 by 10.)
1949. Inventory of patients' effects. (4 quires, 14 by 8.)
1950. Record of and receipt for moneys and valuables of patients. (3 quires, 8 by 11.)
1951. Record of subsistence and other supplies. (4 quires, 14 by 8.)
1952. Inventory of furniture, &c. (4 quires, 14 by 8.)
1953. Inventory of medical supplies, &c. (2 quires, 14 by 8.)
1954. Record of liquors consumed. (3 quires, 10 by 8.)
1955. Medical officers' journal. (3 quires, 14 by 8.)
1956. Record of medical inspections of seamen. (6 quires, 14 by 8.)
1957. Record of letters and papers received. (3 quires, 11 by 8.)
1958. Record of letters and papers sent. (3 quires, 11 by 8.)
1962. Blank book, plain. (3 quires, 16 by 10.)
1963. Blank book, 8½ by 5½ inches, sheep cover, 100 leaves, ruled for dollars and cents.
1964. Blank book, 7 by 5 inches, sheep cover, 60 leaves, ruled for dollars and cents.

# STATIONERY.

Bill paper.
Cap paper.
Legal-cap paper.
Letter paper, ruled.
Letter paper, headed, indorsed, half sheets.
Letter paper, ruled and indorsed, half sheets.
Note paper, headed, whole sheets.
Envelope paper.
Manila paper.
Card blotter.
Envelopes, No. 9½.
Envelopes, No. 8½.
Envelopes, No. 5.
Black lead pencils.
Red and blue pencils.
Rubber bands, No. 30.
Rubber bands, No. 31.
Rubber bands, No. 32.
Rubber bands, No. 33.
Rubber bands, No. 45.
Rubber bands, No. 00¼.
Rubber bands, No. 00½.
Rubber bands, No. 00¾.
Rubber bands, No. 11.
Steel pens: Gillott's, Nos. 170, 294, 303, 351, 352, 353, 390, 393, 404, 604; Spencerian, 1, 2, 3, 4, 5, 11, 12; Medallion, Perry's, Nos. 27, 28, 36, 120, 127, 140, 336; H. & B. 91; Albata, Falcon, Falcon No. 2, Index, Commercial, Bank, Quill, Amalgam, and Dreka.
Barrel pens, Perry's, 70; 225 in 263, 226 in 227, 262 in 289, 808.
Pen-holders.
McGill's fasteners.
Bond seals.
Cut quills.
Erasers.
Shears.

Iron paper-weights.
Glass inkstands, 2-inch.
Glass inkstands, 3-inch.
Glass inkstands.
Pen-racks.
Gutta-percha rulers, 12-inch.
Box-wood rulers, — inch.
Arm-rests.
Ivory folders.
Tin folders.
Letter-clips, board, letter size.
Letter-clips, small.
Pin-cushions.
Sponge-cups, glass.
Bill-files, upright.
Press-copying brushes.
Red tape.
Shipman's letter-files, letter size.
Pins.
Sponge.
Rubber.
Twine.
Sealing-wax.
Copying-press.
Copying-bowl.
Letter-copying books.
Oiled paper.
Ink-eraser.
Arnold's copying-ink.
French copying-ink.
Carter's ink.
Arnold's fluid.
Thaddeus Davids' black ink.
Carmine, No. 3.
Mucilage, small bottles, with brushes.
Best mucilage.
Memorandum blocks, large.
Memorandum blocks, small.

## OPINION OF FIRST COMPTROLLER OF THE TREASURY DEPARTMENT RELATIVE TO THE QUARANTINE ACT OF 1878.

[Extract.]

1. When an act which repeals a prior act is itself only a temporary act, the general rule is that the prior law is revived after the temporary act expires by its own limitation.

2. Some provisions of the act of April 29, 1878, (20 Stat., 37,) entitled ''An act to prevent the introduction of contagious or infectious diseases into the United States,'' were in terms "repealed" by an act with the same title, approved June 2, 1879, (21 Stat., 5–7;) but section 10 of the latter act declared that "this act shall not continue in force for a longer period than four years from the date of its approval.'' Held, that in view of the language and purpose of said acts, the repealed provisions of the act of April 29, 1878, (20 Stat., 37,) revived on June 2, 1883, and are now in force.

When a repealing act expires by its own limitation, it cannot be said to be ''repealed'' within the meaning of section 12 of the Revised Statutes. This section, therefore, has no application to the acts of April 29, 1878, and June 2, 1879. The effect of the expiration of the act of June 2, 1879, is left to be controlled (1) by the legislative intent, ascertained by the usual rules of construction, and (2) by common-law principles, so far as they are not modified by the circumstances showing a different legislative intent. Common-law principles unaffected by such circumstances generally give to the expiration of a repealing act the force which the common law assigns to an express repeal of such repealing act. And the acts of April 29, 1878, and June 2, 1879, when read and considered together in connection with the purpose apparent therein, sufficiently show a legislative intent to revive the provisions of the act of April 29, 1878, temporarily suspended by the act of June 2, 1879. Many of the unrepealed provisions of the act of April 29, 1878, require for their operative effect the agencies and powers found either in the suspended provision thereof or in the act of June 2, 1879. And it is wholly inadmissible to conceive that Congress intended that the main purposes provided for in the act of April 29, 1878, which were not suspended or changed, should be either inefficient or practically inoperative, as they would be if both suspended provisions of this act of April 29, 1878, and the provisions of the act of June 2, 1879, all permanently ceased to be operative. (Lawrence, First Comptroller's decision, (1883,) iv, 436–442.)

# INDEX.

8 R R

# INDEX.

## D.

## E.

# F.

# G.

# H.

## I.

## L.

## M.

## N.

## O.

Relief—*Continued.*

## S.

## T.

## U.

www.ingramcontent.com/pod-product-compliance
Lightning Source LLC
Chambersburg PA
CBHW030624270326
41927CB00007B/1294